BADGER ASSEMBLY

with Christian themes

Ages 5-7

Andy & Barbara Seed, Sally Maynard

Contents

© Badger Learning

Introduction

There are twenty five assemblies for children aged five to seven in this book, all with Christian themes. Each assembly begins with an introduction and then a main presentation, usually given by the teacher. There are both interactive and non-interactive follow-up ideas and every assembly concludes with an optional reflection or prayer. The assemblies use a wide range of stimulus material:

- Bible stories
- Original stories
- Poems and excerpts from children's books
- 'True life' stories: factual accounts of people's lives
- Factual accounts of events
- Information, e.g. about the work of Christian organisations
- Mini-drama sketches for children to perform, with playscripts

Follow-up

Each assembly presentation is followed by suggestions for interaction to involve the audience in the assembly, and to reinforce learning. Interactive follow-up activities include:

- Closed and open questions
- Active response, e.g. vote, hands up, thumbs up or down
- Choral responses: finishing off statements
- Use of volunteers to assist at the front
- Discussion

Non-interactive follow-up suggestions include: a summary of the story; points to think about; reflection and prayer.

Using the material

The assemblies in the book are designed to be used flexibly: it is intended that teachers select the most appropriate follow-up activities and questions from the range provided to meet the needs of the children present. The basic core presentation of each assembly may also be adapted to suit the school, of course, and may be used, for example, in circle time as the basis for role-play or other drama or for classroom discussion. Questions to stimulate response from the children might include:

- What might it feel like to be in this situation?
- Have you experienced a situation like this in real life?
- Why did the characters do what they did?
- Were they right/wrong?

What makes a successful assembly?

Good preparation is essential, particularly if drama is involved. Other key pointers:

- Use of props or a visual focus (suggestions are included in the book; don't forget a data projector can be used if you can't find the object suggested).
- Relate the contents of the assembly to activities going on in the school or community.
- Interactivity: music, songs, drama or any kind of audience participation generates interest.
- Use the story or presentation to make a single clear learning point, which can be reinforced in the reflection or prayer at the end of the assembly.

© Badger Learning

1 Moses in the Basket

Objective
To help children understand one of the most well-known Old Testament stories.

RE themes
Judaism, The Torah, Bible stories, Old Testament, Moses.

Props
(Not essential): a basket big enough to hold a baby.

Introduction
Today, there are many Jewish people in the world. But a very long time ago, the Jews were nearly completely destroyed. It took a very brave woman and a basket to save them, and God, of course: here's the story.

Bible Story: Moses in the Basket (Bible ref: Exodus 2:1-10)

A great many ages ago, before machines and roads and books, the people of Israel, the Hebrews, lived in a foreign land called Egypt. The people of Israel were God's special people and He wanted to give them a land of their own. First they had to leave the country of Egypt, but this they could not do because they were slaves.

The king of Egypt was called Pharaoh and he was worried about the people of Israel. 'There are so many of them that one day they might take over our country. We must put them to work as slaves.' And so the Egyptian masters put the people of Israel to work as slaves: they built cities and monuments and they farmed the land, and the work was hard and endless.

Even though the people of Israel were treated cruelly, God still looked after them, and each family had lots of strong, healthy children. Pharaoh noticed this and saw that their numbers grew and grew. 'I must stop them or these Hebrews will overthrow us,' he thought.

Pharaoh tried all sorts of things to stop the people of Israel becoming a larger and larger nation, but nothing seemed to work. In the end he came up with a plan that was evil and terrible and cruel. He ordered his soldiers to throw every Hebrew baby boy into the River Nile.

Now, at this time, there was a Hebrew woman called Jochabed who was expecting a baby. When the baby was born it turned out to be a boy. She called him Moses, and then she hid him away, fearing that the Egyptian soldiers would find him and take him away. It was a very risky thing to do and after three months she knew that she had to do something else or she would be found out.

Jochabed prayed to God to save Moses, her baby boy. Then she wrapped him in cloths and placed him in a basket. She covered the outside of the basket with sticky black tar, which is waterproof, and she took it down to the banks of the River Nile. It was a desperately hard thing for a mother to do, but Jochabed knew that it was her only hope of saving her son. She prayed that he would be safe from the crocodiles and boats, and she asked God to watch over him until he was safely in the hands of a caring person. Then, slowly and carefully, she placed the basket containing little Moses onto the water and gave it a push. As she watched it float away, she wiped her eyes and turned back for home.

Now later on that day, a mile or so downstream, the Pharaoh's daughter, a princess, was bathing in the river as she did every day. Out of the corner of her eye she saw a dark shape in the reeds and heard a sound. "It sounds like a baby crying," she thought to herself. The princess ordered one of her slaves to have a look. The woman brought the basket to the princess who looked inside and then lifted out baby Moses. He was crying with hunger. "The poor little thing," she said. "This is one of the Hebrew babies." And she immediately felt sorry for him.

Now, as it happened, Moses had an older sister who was another slave of the princess. She knew that this was her baby brother that had been found and so she went over to the princess. "Shall I get one of the Hebrew women to nurse the baby for you?"

"Yes," said Pharaoh's daughter. "That's a good idea, go." So Moses' sister went to fetch his mother. And so the princess asked Jochabed to look after her own son for her, and what is more, she paid her to do it too.

Moses grew up in the royal palace of Pharaoh and became a prince of Egypt. And later on, when he grew into a man, God set him in place as the leader of the Hebrews, the one who took them out of slavery and back to the promised land of Israel.

Interactive Follow-Up Activities

Questions
1. Why was Pharaoh worried about the Hebrews? *(There were so many of them; he thought that they might take over Egypt).*
2. Why did Jochabed put baby Moses in a basket on the River Nile? *(To save him from Pharaoh's soldiers, who were killing every Hebrew baby boy).*
3. What happened to Moses? *(He was found by a princess, and brought up by his own mother).*

Getting the message

1. Why did God look after Moses? *(Because later on as a man, he would lead the people out of Egypt to the promised land).*
2. Why did the Hebrews want to leave Egypt? *(They were slaves, treated cruelly; God had promised them their own land: Israel).*
3. Hands up:
   - Who thinks Pharaoh was cruel to the Hebrews?
   - Who thinks Jochabed, the mother of Moses was very brave?
   - Who thinks it was just lucky that the princess found Moses in the basket?
   - Who thinks God kept Moses safe?
   - Who thinks it is right that some people are slaves?

Non-interactive Follow-Up

Summary of the story

- The Hebrews lived in Egypt after the time of Joseph.
- Pharaoh was worried because their numbers were so great.
- The Israelites became slaves and were treated harshly.
- Pharaoh ordered that all Hebrew baby boys should be thrown in the river.
- Jochabed, a Hebrew woman, put her baby boy Moses in a waterproof basket on the Nile and prayed for his safety.
- He was found by the Pharaoh's daughter, a princess.
- Moses was nursed by his own mother and went on to become an important prince, and later the man who led the Hebrews out of slavery and towards the promised land.

Reflection

We should be grateful that we live in times when slavery is against the law and where kings and queens cannot order children to be harmed. Let us be thankful for the peaceful times that we live in.

Prayer

Lord God, thank You for the story of Moses. Thank You that we no longer live in times when many people are kept as slaves and treated in cruel ways. But please look after those people around the world who are suffering cruel treatment at this time. Set them free, like You set the Hebrews free from Egypt. Amen.

[Note: The Ten Plagues assembly follows on the story from this assembly].

2 Daniel in the Lions' Den

Objective
To introduce children to the stories of the Old Testament.

RE themes
Judaism, The Torah, Bible stories, Old Testament, Daniel, beliefs and practice, prayer.

Props
(Not essential); lion masks; crowns; small whiteboard and markers; goblets.

Introduction
Would you fancy being put in a pit full of lions and left there? This is the story of a man who was and how he was protected....

Bible Story: Daniel in the Lions' Den

There was once a king called Belshazzar who was related to a famous king called Nebuchadnezzar. When Nebuchadnezzar was king he had a servant called Daniel who often helped him to understand the many strange dreams that he had. One day King Belshazzar decided to give a huge feast for over 1,000 people. They had magnificent food and delicious wine. Belshazzar decided that as it was such a special feast, he wanted to drink his wine from special goblets and he ordered his servants to bring the gold cups that Nebuchadnezzar had stolen from the temple in Jerusalem. His servants did as they were told and soon everyone was drinking from the gold goblets and praising their gods, which were made from gold, silver, bronze and iron.

They were all very merry, but suddenly everyone froze and looked at the wall – a hand had appeared and the fingers were writing words. Everybody watched as the words appeared – King Belshazzar turned white and his knees knocked together. He started to call for magicians, wise men – anyone who he thought might be able to read what had been written on the walls. "I will give a reward," he said, "to anyone who can read this and explain it. I will give him royal clothes made of purple cloth and gold chain, and I will make him the third highest ruler in the kingdom." The magicians and wise men came, but they could not explain the words to the king. Belshazzar became more and more afraid, but when his mother arrived, she told him that there was a man in the kingdom who could tell him what the words meant. "His name is Daniel," she said, "and he has the spirit of the Holy God in him. Call for him, he will be able to help you."

So Daniel came and explained the writing. "Nebuchadnezzar started as a good and wise ruler, but then he became selfish and greedy. So he was removed as king. And you, Belshazzar, have drunk from cups that you knew had been stolen and you have worshipped idols. The Lord God is not pleased with you and this will be your punishment: your kingdom is coming to an end, you have been judged unworthy.

You will be killed and your land will be divided amongst the Medes and the Persians." Daniel's words came true that very night and Darius became the next king.

Darius was a good man and liked Daniel very much, but there were other bad men who didn't like Daniel at all and they plotted to have him killed. They tricked Darius into making a law. This law said that no one could pray to anyone but Darius for 30 days. Anyone who prayed to God would be thrown into the lions' den. But Daniel still prayed to God. The bad men told Darius and so he was forced to throw Daniel into the lions' den. Darius could not sleep that night and the next day he hurried to the lions' den to see what had happened to Daniel.

He called to Daniel: "Daniel! Has the God you worship been able to save you from the lions?"

Daniel answered him: "I prayed to God and He sent his angels to close the lions' mouths – they have not hurt me because I have done nothing wrong."

Darius was so relieved and pleased that he told his people how Daniel had been saved from the lions and said that from now on he and his people would worship Daniel's God.

Interactive Follow-Up Activities

Questions
1. How was Daniel saved from the lions? *(He prayed and God closed the mouths of the lions so they would not harm Daniel).*
2. Who was the king who stole the goblets from the temple in Jerusalem? *(Nebuchadnezzar).*
3. What happened when everybody was drinking and feasting at the banquet? *(A hand appeared and started writing on the wall).*
4. What else were the people doing apart from drinking and eating? *(They were worshipping gold, silver, bronze and iron gods).*

Getting the message
1. Why was King Belshazzar so frightened? *(Because he didn't know what the writing meant).*
2. Why did he call for Daniel? *(Because his mother told him Daniel had helped King Nebuchadnezzar understand his dreams).*
3. Why do you think God saved Daniel? *(Because he had done nothing wrong; he had stayed faithful to God and refused to worship anyone or anything else; because he prayed for help).*

Non-interactive Follow-Up

Summary of the story

- Belshazzar had a feast for 1,000 people and asked his servants to use goblets that been stolen from the temple in Jerusalem by Nebuchadnezzar.
- During the feast a hand appeared and writing appeared on a wall.
- Daniel told the king what the writing meant and the king was killed that night.
- The new King Darius was tricked into making a law that said people could only pray to him, but Daniel refused and continued to pray to his God.
- Darius had no choice but to throw Daniel to the lions but he was saved because God closed the mouths of the lions so that they wouldn't harm him.
- The king decreed that everyone should worship Daniel's God.

Reflection

Even though Daniel knew he was in danger, he refused to obey a law that was wrong. He was faithful to God, and God saved him by protecting him from the lions.

Prayer

Lord God, thank You for the story of Daniel, which shows us how to trust You even when things look hopeless. Help us to pray to You every day, not just when we are in trouble or need help. Amen.

Objective
To teach children that Jesus needed friends and disciples to help him to tell people about the Kingdom of God. To help them to reflect on how important friends are.

RE themes
Christianity, Bible stories, New Testament, Jesus, disciples.

Props
A child's fishing net.

Introduction
Who's ever used one of these at the seaside to catch crabs and tiny fish in rock pools? Well this sort of net wouldn't have been much good to the person in our story today. His fishing nets were much, much bigger. I'll let him tell you all about an amazing fishing trip that happened about 2,000 years ago....

Bible Story: The Big Catch (Bible ref: Luke 5: 1 – 11)

Hello! My name's Simon. That's my fishing boat down by the edge of the lake, over there. You wouldn't believe what happened to my friends and me yesterday. It was so amazing that I can hardly believe it myself! Let me tell you all about it.

I was out fishing with James and John the night before last. We're fishermen on the Sea of Galilee, you see. We often go out fishing when it's dark. It's beautiful out on the water at night: the air is wonderfully still and the moonbeams seem to dance on the water. You can see the fish swimming all round the boat. The moonlight makes them look like little silver arrows darting about in the black water. We often get our biggest catches at night time. But not that night, we didn't.

We went to all of the places we know that the fish love to hide, but we didn't catch a single one. We kept letting the nets down over the side of the boat, and each time we pulled them up again, they were just as empty as before. We carried on doing that for hours and hours, and in the end we just gave up. It was as if every fish in the whole lake had completely disappeared.

The sun had just come up as we sailed towards the land. We were tired and hungry, and just wanted to get home. Sadly for us, we still had one more job to do before we could get any sleep. We still had to wash our nets before we put them away. As we washed them, we could see a crowd of people sitting listening to a man talking to them. We recognised the man – it was Jesus. He's a carpenter, you know, but he's been going round this area, telling everyone all about God, as well as healing people who are ill. (I know all about him because he came to my house one day and made my wife's mother better, when she'd been so poorly we were worried she might die).

Anyway, we'd just finished washing the nets, when Jesus came over to our boats. He got into my boat, and spoke to the people on the shore from there: it was as if he was standing on a sort of stage. When he'd finished what he had to say, he said to me;

"Simon, take the boat out into the deep water, and let down your nets for a catch of fish."

I groaned at the thought of going out fishing again. My hands were still full of blisters from the night's fishing. "Master, we've worked hard all night and haven't caught anything," I grumbled. I really didn't want to bother! But then I remembered how Jesus had made my wife's mother better, and how he'd made blind people see and deaf people hear; he also looked at me in a way that made me really want to do as he asked, no matter how tired I was. So I carried on:

"But because it's you who's asked me, I'll let down the nets again." And that's just what we did.

You'll never guess what happened next! When we pulled the nets up, they weren't empty like they had been all night. No. They were full to bursting with the biggest, hugest, most ENORMOUS catch of fish we'd ever seen! There were so many fish that the nets started to break, and the boat began to sink. Luckily there were some other fishermen nearby in their boat, and they helped us to get the fish back to the shore. Nobody had ever seen a catch of fish like that one! I bet people will be talking about that catch for years to come!

As we were taking the boat to land, I suddenly felt very peculiar. I looked at Jesus and realised that all these fish were somehow to do with him. He'd known that all the fish had disappeared during the night when we were looking for them; he'd known that that the fish would be there out in that deep water at exactly that time; in fact I wondered whether he hadn't actually made it happen! Could that be possible? I fell down on the ground right there in front of him, in amazement. I was more than a bit scared – especially when I thought back to how he'd healed all those people as well. Jesus certainly wasn't an ordinary man!

And do you know what? After that, we got out of our boats and left all of our expensive fishing gear right there on the shore. We left them and decided to follow him wherever he was going to go. If God can help him do amazing stuff like that, then we want to know more about Him, and we want to tell other people too. I've got a funny feeling that James, John and me won't be doing much fishing on that lake any more. I think our lives have just changed forever!

Interactive Follow-Up Activities

Questions

1. What job did Simon, James and John have? *(They were fishermen).*
2. What special thing had Jesus done at Simon's house? *(He had healed his mother-in-law).*
3. What was Jesus doing before he got into Simon's boat? *(He was telling people all about God).*
4. Why was Simon scared when he saw the huge catch of fish? *(He realised that Jesus was not an ordinary man, and that the catch of fish, like the healings he'd seen, were miraculous).*
5. Why do you think that Simon, James and John decided to follow Jesus? *(They realised that God had helped Jesus to do these amazing things, and they wanted to learn more about Him, and to tell other people about it all).*

Getting the message

1. Jesus wanted as many people as possible to hear all about God. He needed ways to spread the good news that God loved them and wanted to help them in their lives. We know that he did manage to spread the good news, because we're still talking about it today. But how did the news get spread? Give a thumbs-up to the ideas that would have worked in Jesus' time and a big thumbs-down to ideas that wouldn't have worked then:
   a. Jesus rang up the TV station and got them to do an advert.
   b. Jesus told all of his friends, and they went and told lots more people *(thumbs-up: the disciples).*
   c. Jesus told his story to a reporter from the *Daily Mail* newspaper.
   d. People who Jesus knew wrote down everything that happened for other people to read *(thumbs-up: the Gospels).*
2. Jesus chose a group of special friends to help him with his work. *(This special group of men that followed him and learned all about God's ways from Jesus were called his disciples).* Why do you think he started by choosing Simon, James and John? *(Open-ended; could include that he knew they were hard workers, that they would do what he asked them to do, that they had seen some of his miracles first hand, etc.).*

Non-interactive Follow-Up

Summary of the story

- Simon, James and John had fished all night, and not caught anything.
- Jesus was teaching a crowd all about God at the side of the lake.
- Jesus got into Simon's boat.
- He asked Simon to go back out onto the lake and try fishing again.
- Simon didn't want to because he was tired, but did it because Jesus had asked him.
- They caught a huge amount of fish.
- Simon, James and John left everything to follow Jesus and decided to tell other people all about Him.

Reflection

Even though Jesus was the Son of God, He still needed friends to help Him. Think about what might have happened if Simon, James and John had decided not to follow Jesus on that day. We might never have heard all about Jesus and the amazing miracles that He did. Also, He didn't only need His friends to tell people about God. Without good friends Jesus would have been very lonely indeed.

Prayer

Lord God, thank You that Jesus had such good news to tell people about You: that You love us all and that You can make our lives better. Help us to learn more about what Jesus taught His friends and the people who lived near the Sea of Galilee. Thank You also that You know how important it is for us to have friends to help us. Please help us to be good friends. Amen.

4 | The Boy Who Left Home

Objective
To help children explore what happens when we make mistakes or take wrong decisions. To help them understand the importance of forgiveness.

RE themes
Christianity, Bible stories, New Testament, Jesus, parables, forgiveness.

Props
(Not essential): a toy pig and a smart/colourful cloak of some sort.
(The story is told in two parts, with an interactive session in between them).

Introduction
Has anyone here ever made a mistake? I bet you have – I know I've made plenty in my life! All of us make mistakes and sometimes we even do bad things. But what happens if you make a really BIG mistake? What can you do to sort it out? This story is about a boy who made a whopping great mistake. It starts in a smelly pigpen, way out in the countryside.

Story: The Boy Who Left Home

Hugo (show the pig and then place in a prominent position, if using props) was a happy pig, with a huge great tummy and a lovely muddy pigpen to live in. It was a beautiful sunny day, and he'd just had an enormous dinner of delicious pods to eat. He had settled down for a quiet snooze in the sun, when he was disturbed by a grumbling, muttering sort of noise.

"Oh Hugo," sighed a voice. "You just don't know how lucky you are." The voice belonged to the boy who looked after the pigs in the pigpen, and who brought them their food. Hugo liked the boy, so he grunted an understanding sort of piggy grunt, and the boy carried on talking. "I've got no money to buy food, and I haven't eaten anything for days. I'm so hungry, that I could even eat some of those disgusting-looking pods from your trough. How on earth did I get myself into this mess?"

Hugo moved, to let the boy tickle his tummy, and looked as if he were listening carefully to what the boy was saying.

"It all started a long while ago, when I was still living at home, in my father's house. I worked hard every day. I had everything I needed – plenty of food and a comfortable bed – but I wasn't satisfied with my life. I wanted to travel the world and have fun instead. So one day, I asked my father for my share of his money, and told him I wanted to leave home. My father was very sad, but he let me have my own way. He gave me a lot of money, and off I went into the big wide world. My brother stayed at home to carry on working for my dad.

"At first it was brilliant. I had plenty of money for expensive food and parties, and I made lots of new friends. Soon, though, things went badly wrong. I ran out of money, and all my new friends didn't seem to like me any more. I got hungry and cold, and had nowhere to live. That's when I met you, Hugo." Hugo flapped a lazy ear and turned over so that the boy could scratch his back now.

"A farmer gave me a job looking after you, but he doesn't pay me enough to buy proper food. I bet even my dad's servants get more food than I do!" The boy sighed another big sigh. "What on earth can I do, Hugo?"

He decided that he would go back to his father's house. He knew that he'd done wrong in wasting all of his money, and that his father was going to be very angry indeed. He decided to say that he was really sorry. He planned to ask his dad if he could work in his house as a servant, instead of being like a son to him. He wasn't sure that his dad would forgive him.

Interactive Follow-Up Activities

Questions
1. Where did the boy used to live? *(At home with his father and brother)*.
2. What did he decide to do? *(He decided to go and travel the world and have fun instead of staying at home to work)*.
3. Can you remember what happened to all the money that the boy's father gave him? *(He spent it on expensive parties)*.

What happened next?

Now, I need someone to come up and pretend to be the boy *(choose a volunteer)*. Let's give him a name – what about 'Zak'?

What do you think will happen when Zak goes home? Put your hand up if you've got a good idea. *(Pick a few children to give their ideas: dad may be cross and send him away; dad may forgive him; he might chicken out and not dare to go home after all, etc.)*.

Stay here, Zak, and we'll see what happens next. *(Stand child at the front while the rest of the story is told)*.

Zak said goodbye to Hugo, and set off home. Before he'd even got near his father's house, he spotted his dad looking out for him. His father ran towards him and gave him a big hug. His dad could see how sorry he was before he'd even managed to get the words out properly. He gave Zak his best cloak *(put cloak onto Zak's shoulders)* and got a huge feast ready to welcome him home. He felt so much better now that his son was home safe and sound.

But Zak's brother Simon was very cross and jealous, because he'd stayed at home and worked while Zak had been wasting all that money. He didn't feel like forgiving his brother and certainly didn't feel like celebrating one bit. He had a really horrible, grumpy evening.

In a pigpen far away, Hugo rolled over in the straw, and wondered how the boy who used to feed him was getting on. Just before he drifted off to sleep in his clean bed, Zak thought to himself, "My dad's really amazing: he loves me, even though I don't deserve it!"

More Questions

4. How do you know that Zak's dad had missed him? *(He was out looking for him).*
5. Why do you think that Zak's brother Simon had a horrible, grumpy evening, instead of enjoying the party? *(Because he hadn't forgiven his brother for wasting all of the money on parties while he stayed at home and worked).*

Non-interactive Follow-Up

Summary of the story

- Zak is hungry and poor and looks after pigs.
- He used to live at home and work for his father.
- He decided that he wanted to leave home and travel the world.
- His father was sad, but gave him his share of the family's money.
- Zak wasted the money on wild living and parties.
- He realises he was wrong and goes home to say he's sorry.
- His father is very pleased to have him back and forgives him, but his brother is still angry with him.

Something to think about

1. Think of a time when you made a big mistake or did something bad.
2. Did you say that you were sorry?
3. Why is it important to say that you're sorry if you do something bad?
4. Is it important to forgive someone if they say sorry to you?

Reflection

Zak did some bad things, such as wasting his father's money on wild parties. He ended up so miserable that he didn't know what to do. When he was truly sorry, he found out how much his father loved him and forgave him, even though he didn't really deserve it. That made him feel so much better. Try to remember that saying sorry is a good way to make you feel better.

Prayer

Lord God, thank You that You love us and care for us, even when we make mistakes or do bad things. Please help us to say that we're sorry when we have done something bad. Thank You that You forgive us as soon as we've said sorry, just like the father in the story. Help us to forgive other people, when they say sorry to us.

Objective

To enable children to understand the Christian belief that Jesus was not an ordinary man, but had power over nature.

RE themes

Christianity, Bible stories, New Testament, Jesus, miracles.

Props

(None).

Introduction

Jesus had lots of friends and lots of followers called disciples. They knew He was not an ordinary man because He said such wise things and He was able to heal people. But one day they found out something quite amazing about Him.

Bible Story: The Storm That Went Away

(Bible ref: Mark 4:35-41)

Jesus was tired. All day he'd been standing and talking to a great crowd of people by the Lake in Galilee, telling them stories about the Kingdom of God. Jesus used stories to tell people the right way to live and how to please God, and there were always hundreds who wanted to listen to him.

But now the sun was setting and evening was on its way. Jesus pointed to Peter the fisherman's boat and said, "Come on friends, let's go over to the other side of the lake." So Jesus climbed into the boat, along with his twelve special friends: Peter, Andrew, James, John, Philip, Bartholemew, Matthew, James son of Alphaeus, Judas, Simon, Thomas and Judas Iscariot.

Jesus went to the back of the boat and lay down on the fishing nets to rest. Peter and James pushed the small wooden boat away from the shore and the watching people, then set the sails ready for the journey. Immediately, a gust of wind filled the sails and started them moving out into the deep waters of the huge lake known as the Sea of Galilee.

Some of the men noticed that Jesus was already asleep. "He must be worn out," said Andrew. "He's been teaching the crowds for days without a break."

"Where does he get all those amazing stories from?" said Thomas.

"He says they're from his father," said James.

"And what about all those people he healed in the last few weeks before we came here?" said Andrew.

"Yes, he cured my mother-in-law's fever just by praying for her. My wife thought she was going to die – it truly was a miracle," said Peter.

"And don't forget that man who had leprosy," said James. "The one whose skin was in a terrible condition."

"That's right," said Thomas. "Jesus just touched him and his skin became clean. I wouldn't have believed it if I hadn't seen it with my own eyes."

The twelve disciples of Jesus talked about him for hours as they steered the boat across the lake. They recalled the paralysed man who could now walk and many others who had been cured of all sorts of problems. They talked about who Jesus was and whether he was really God's son. Then, as they came towards the centre of the lake, two of the men were suddenly thrown off their feet as the little boat lurched to one side.

"Wow, that was a big wave," said Peter. "Are you two alright?" But before the men could answer, a strong gust of wind ripped into the sail, causing such a noise that the disciples all grabbed hold of the boat's side with fright.

"We must take the sail down or it will tear!" shouted Peter. "There's a storm on its way." Peter was right, but he hadn't realised that the storm was already upon them. Then, without warning, another great wave crashed into the front of the boat, coming high over the sides and soaking everything. Once more the boat was thrown upwards and James grabbed the mast to stop himself falling into the sea. His feet were ankle-deep in bitterly cold water.

The twelve men were now praying and in fear of their lives. They all knew people who had drowned in the lake during these sudden storms. Andrew scrambled to the back of the boat to see if Jesus was alright. As he did so, a ferocious bolt of lightning cut across the black clouds, immediately followed by a fearsome rumble of thunder. In the brief flash of light, Andrew could see that Jesus was still asleep in the back of the boat. He couldn't believe it. He shook Jesus awake. "Teacher, don't you care if we drown?"

Jesus stood up and looked at the great waves all around. Then he held out his hand into the wind and spoke a command. "Quiet!" The surging wind immediately died down. To the waves Jesus ordered, "Be still!" Within a few seconds the waves died down to a gentle swell. The sea was calm and quiet.

Andrew and the other men were terrified. They were so amazed that they didn't know what to say. Jesus spoke to them. "Why are you so afraid? Do you still have no faith?"

The disciples looked amongst themselves and said, "Who is this man? Even the wind and the waves obey him!"

Interactive Follow-Up Activities

Questions

1. What had Jesus been doing before he got into the boat? *(Healing people and telling them stories/teaching them).*
2. Why did Jesus fall asleep in the boat? *(He was tired after talking to crowds of people for days).*
3. What happened on the lake? *(There was a sudden storm; the disciples thought they were going to drown; they woke Jesus up and he calmed the storm miraculously).*

Getting the message

1. What did the twelve disciples think about Jesus before the storm?
   (They thought he was an amazing man; they knew he had power to heal and he was a great teacher).
2. What did the twelve disciples think of Jesus after the storm? *(They were afraid of him because they realised that he even had power over nature; they knew he was no ordinary man).*
3. Ask for a volunteer to come out and play the part of Jesus. Then get the audience to mime the water of the lake using their hands, calm at first and then becoming rough with large waves. Jesus can reach out his hands and command the waves to die down.
4. Finish off each sentence by calling out the right word:
   - Jesus and his disciples sailed across the lake in a small _____. *(boat)*
   - Jesus fell asleep because he was very _____. *(tired)*
   - A sudden storm came with a strong wind and big _____. *(waves)*
   - The disciples woke up _____. *(Jesus)*
   - Jesus told the wind to be _____. *(quiet)*
   - Jesus commanded the waves to die _____. *(down)*
   - The disciples were very _____. *(afraid)*

Non-interactive Follow-Up

Summary of the story

- Jesus was tired after teaching big crowds of people by the Sea of Galilee for days.
- He suggested to His twelve disciples that they cross the lake in a small fishing boat.
- Jesus fell asleep and the men talked about all the things that Jesus did, including miraculous healings.
- A sudden storm came and waves swept over the boat: the men thought they were going to drown.
- They woke Jesus, who commanded the wind and waves to be still.
- The storm died down immediately and the men were afraid of Jesus because of His amazing power.
- Jesus questioned their faith in Him.

Reflection

Christians believe that Jesus was no ordinary man but that He was the Son of God and had great power. The Bible says He was able to made sick people better and He was even able to calm a storm. Jesus performed many other great miracles too – this is why millions of people all over the world still worship Him today.

Prayer

Lord God, thank You for the wonderful story of how Your Son Jesus calmed the storm on the Sea of Galilee, two thousand years ago. He showed the twelve disciples that He was not an ordinary man but someone with great power. Please care for us in the storms of life, just as You cared for the twelve men in the little fishing boat. Amen.

Objective

To teach children that everyone can change their ways.

RE themes

Christianity, Bible stories, New Testament, Jesus, belonging.

Props

(None).

Introduction

In films there are always goodies and baddies. But are goodies always good and baddies always bad? Here's a story from the Bible about someone who changed.

Bible Story: The Man in the Tree (Bible ref: Luke 19:1-9)

Nobody in the town of Jericho liked Zacchaeus. Zacchaeus was mean. Zacchaeus was nasty. Zacchaeus was always taking the people's money away from them. Zacchaeus was a cheat, too.

His job was tax collector for the Romans. This meant that everybody had to give him a quarter of their money each month. A quarter! Most people had too little to feed their families as it was. But Zacchaeus was mean, as I said. If you didn't pay, he would tell the Roman soldiers to come round and smash up your house. But worst of all, he used to ask for more money than he was supposed to. If the Romans wanted five silver coins from Jacob the Potter, Zacchaeus would ask for six, but if Jacob complained, Zacchaeus would tell the Romans he was a troublemaker and then, well, it could get nasty.

Zacchaeus lived in a big house on the edge of town. He ate the best food and he had servants to cook it and bring it to him. He had beautiful furniture and rich clothes. He could afford it because he had lots of the people's money, and they really didn't like him at all.

Well, do you know, a funny thing happened in Jericho one day. Word got around that there was a real miracle worker coming through the town, a man who could heal sick people. Just the day before, he had helped a blind man to see. His name was Jesus. They said he was a wonderful storyteller and the kindest man that ever lived. Well, of course, every single person in the town wanted to see this man, and when he arrived at midday, there were huge crowds everywhere lining the streets. Everyone was talking about him.

"Why has he come here?"

"What's he going to do?"

"I hope we see a miracle."

"He might heal my poorly father."

"Where will he stay?"

"Who's going to feed him?"

"Some say that he's really the Son of God."

"He just looks like an ordinary fellow to me."

Now Zacchaeus had also heard that Jesus was in town and he too wanted to see this man, the doer of miracles. But when Zacchaeus went out into the streets, they were so crowded that he couldn't see a thing.

"Let me through!" he shouted. "Let me see him." But for once nobody took any notice of Zacchaeus. Even when he found a place which wasn't so crowded, Zacchaeus still couldn't see because he was a very short man. He looked around for some steps or somewhere to get higher up, but everywhere was taken. Then he saw a tree by the side of the road. Zacchaeus rushed over and began to climb. The people nearby couldn't believe their eyes – many of them laughed: they never expected to see the important tax collector climbing a tree to see a man who was only the son of a carpenter, after all.

When Jesus came around the corner, the people cheered and crowded round him. Zacchaeus could just about see the top of his head in the distance. "At least he's coming this way," Zacchaeus said to himself as he clung onto the branches wondering whether he had torn his expensive cloak. Well, Jesus did go that way, and not only that, but he stopped underneath the tree and looked up.

"Zacchaeus, come down immediately," said Jesus. "I must stay at your house today." Zacchaeus couldn't believe it, and nor could the watching people. "But how did he know my name?" thought Zacchaeus as he scrambled down the tree with a silly grin on his face. Meanwhile the people were muttering.

"Jesus is going to stay with the tax collector?"

"But he's a cheat and a robber that man."

"Why has he gone to stay with him of all people? Why not me – I'm an honest man."
"This is ridiculous."

But off Jesus went to Zacchaeus' house where he was given food to eat and a chance to rest. When Jesus left the house, there were still crowds of people outside and they were still muttering, but it was Zacchaeus who made them quiet.

"People of Jericho – please listen. Today, I, Zacchaeus, am giving half of all that I own to the poor people of this town. And if I have cheated anyone, I will pay back four times the amount."

A great cheer went up from the crowd. They couldn't believe it. Then Jesus spoke up.

"Rejoice because this shows that anyone can change from evil to good."

And Zacchaeus kept his word.

Interactive Follow-Up Activities

Questions
1. Why didn't the people like Zacchaeus? *(He took their money and cheated them)*.
2. Why did everyone want to see Jesus? *(They had heard he could do miracles and heal people)*.
3. How did Zacchaeus manage to see Jesus? *(He climbed a tree)*.

Getting the message
1. Why do you think Jesus chose to stay with Zacchaeus, even though the people hated him? *(Jesus wanted Zacchaeus to change, to show the people that anyone could change; Jesus had time for everybody, even 'bad' people; Zacchaeus needed help)*.
2. What else can we learn from this story? *(That anyone can change; that cheating is wrong; that Jesus helped all sorts of people)*.
3. Ask for a volunteer to come out and be interviewed as Zacchaeus. Alternatively, play the tax collector yourself and invite questions from the audience.

Non-interactive Follow-Up

Summary of the story
- Zacchaeus was a tax collector for the Romans in the town of Jericho.
- He was very unpopular with the people because he cheated them out of money.
- He was rich.
- One day, Jesus the miracle worker came through the town.
- Everyone turned out to see him so that the streets were crowded.
- Zacchaeus was a short man and so he climbed a tree to see Jesus.
- Jesus told Zacchaeus he was staying at his house.
- The people thought it was wrong that Jesus should go to the house of a dishonest man.
- After Jesus spent time with him, Zacchaeus changed completely, announcing that he would give money to the poor and repay those he had cheated.

Reflection

Anyone can change. The story of Zacchaeus shows that someone who has done something wrong can always make the decision to stop it and to start doing what is right. Zacchaeus was sorry for what he had done. If you have done something wrong, remember to say sorry and make sure you try to put it right and don't do it again.

Prayer

Lord God, thank You for the story of Zacchaeus and how he changed completely after he met Jesus. We all do things wrong in our lives, so please help us to say sorry and to do what is right the next time. Amen.

Objective
To introduce children to the concept of the resurrection, which is one of the basic beliefs of Christianity.

RE themes
Christianity, Bible stories, New Testament, Jesus, Easter, beliefs.

Props
(Not essential): picture of tomb with removable stone, guards' helmets, sticks for guards to use as spears, Easter eggs/chocolate.

Introduction
Most of us know about the Easter holiday and chocolate eggs! But do you know why we have a holiday then? This is the story of Jesus, who came back to life again after he was killed....

Bible Story: Jesus is Alive!

When Jesus was on earth he upset quite a few people as well as making lots more very happy. The people he upset most were called the Pharisees – they were teachers in the temple at Jerusalem who thought that he was telling lies and also making them look very silly indeed. They were so upset with him that they plotted to kill him to get rid of him for ever.

Jesus was eventually killed by order of the Roman ruler in Jerusalem, who was called Pilate. When people died in those days they were put to rest in a tomb (or burial place) dug out from the stone and earth – that's if they had enough money. Jesus didn't have any money but a rich man named Joseph of Arimethea asked Pilate for Jesus' body so that he could put him in his own new tomb that he had prepared for himself. Pilate agreed, so Joseph took the body, wrapped it in cloth and put it in the tomb. Pilate was afraid that robbers would try to steal Jesus' body. Jesus had been saying that he would rise on the third day; Pilate wanted to make sure that didn't happen, so he placed guards at the entrance to the tomb, which by then had an enormous stone in front of it. All this happened on what we now call Good Friday (which used to be called God Friday but which over the years has changed to Good Friday).

Two days later, on the Sunday, two women (who were Jesus' friends) went to the tomb to rub oils and spices onto his body, which was the custom of the time. When they arrived, they saw that the stone had been rolled away and the tomb was empty! They were understandably very afraid and confused – but then they saw that they were not alone: an angel was sitting on one of the stones and spoke to them: 'Don't be afraid – Jesus has risen just as he said he would.'

Once they had got over this shock, the women turned again and came face to face with Jesus! Another surprise, but obviously they were overjoyed to see that Jesus was very much alive. He told them to go and tell his disciples what they had seen and to tell them that he would come to them soon. The women went whooping and shouting with happiness to obey Jesus' command to them.

Jesus kept his promise and ate with his disciples by Lake Galilee. He also walked with two men, who didn't recognise him at first, on the road to a place called Emmaus. But after he had eaten with them they realised that it was Jesus. They and all the other people who saw Jesus after he came back to life were overjoyed.

Easter is now a celebration of the Bible stories of Jesus' resurrection and means 'new life'. Some people think that the custom of giving eggs comes from chicks hatching from eggs and coming to life. Others think that maybe the shape of the stone that rolled away from the tomb is a bit like an egg – whatever the reason, it is a very joyful celebration for Christians and is a time of hope.

Interactive Follow-Up Activities

Questions
1. What does resurrection mean? *(Coming back to life)*.
2. Who were the people who hated Jesus the most? *(The Pharisees, who were teachers at the temple in Jerusalem)*.
3. What was the name of the man who asked Pilate if he could put Jesus' body in his own tomb? *(Joseph of Arimethea)*.

Getting the message
1. Why did Pilate put guards in front of Jesus' tomb? *(In case the body was stolen by robbers which might make people think that Jesus had come back to life)*.
2. Why did the two women go the tomb on the Sunday? *(To rub oils and spices onto Jesus' body)*.
3. What do you think the women's first thoughts might have been when they saw:
   * The angel?
   * Jesus?
4. Put up your hand if...
   * You might think more about the reason for the Easter celebration in future.
   * You like Easter eggs!

Non-interactive Follow-Up

Summary of the story

- The Pharisees plotted to kill Jesus.
- After Jesus died, his body was put in a tomb belonging to a rich man called Joseph of Arimethea.
- Pilate, the Roman ruler, ordered guards to be placed in front of the tomb in case the body was stolen.
- When two women arrived on the Sunday to anoint Jesus' body, they found the stone had been rolled away and an angel who told them Jesus had risen from the dead.
- The women then saw Jesus, who told them to go and tell the disciples they had seen Him.
- Jesus appeared to many more people.

Reflection

The Bible says that Jesus came back to life after He died and that if Christians believe in Him, they too will join Him in Heaven and live for ever. This is the message of hope that Christians believe in.

Prayer

Lord God, thank You for Jesus and for the message of hope that He gives us. Help us to live our lives looking to Him as the example we follow. Amen.

Objective
To help children learn the value of being unselfish.

RE themes
Christianity, beliefs and practice: loving others.

Props
(Not essential): A copy of the book *The Selfish Giant* by Oscar Wilde.

Introduction
Everyone knows that being selfish is not good. Today's assembly has the first part of the story of someone who was very selfish and mean.

Story: The Selfish Giant by Oscar Wilde (Part 1)

Every afternoon, as they were coming from school, the children used to go and play in the Giant's garden.

It was a large lovely garden, with soft green grass. Here and there over the grass stood beautiful flowers like stars, and there were twelve peach-trees that in the spring-time broke out into delicate blossoms of pink and pearl, and in the autumn bore rich fruit. The birds sat on the trees and sang so sweetly that the children used to stop their games in order to listen to them. "How happy we are here!" they cried to each other.

One day the Giant came back. He had been to visit his friend the Cornish ogre, and had stayed with him for seven years. After the seven years were over he had said all that he had to say, for his conversation was limited, and he determined to return to his own castle. When he arrived, he saw children playing in the garden.

"What are you doing there?" he cried in a very gruff voice, and the children ran away.

"My own garden is my own garden," said the Giant, "anyone can understand that, and I will allow nobody to play in it but myself." So he built a high wall all round it, and put up a notice board.

TRESPASSERS WILL BE PROSECUTED

He was a very selfish Giant.

The poor children had now nowhere to play. They tried to play on the road, but the road was very dusty and full of hard stones, and they did not like it. They used to wander round the high wall when their lessons were over, and talk about the beautiful garden inside. "How happy we were there," they said to each other.

Then the spring came, and all over the country there were little blossoms and little birds. Only in the garden of the Selfish Giant it was still winter. The birds did not care to sing in it, as there were no children, and the trees forgot to blossom. Once a beautiful flower put its head out from the grass, but when it saw the notice board it was so sorry for the children that it slipped back into the ground again, and went off to sleep. The only people who were pleased were the Snow and the Frost. "Spring has forgotten this garden," they cried, "so we will live here all the year round." The Snow covered up the grass with her great white cloak, and the Frost painted all the trees silver. Then they invited the North Wind to stay with them, and he came. He was wrapped in furs, and he roared all day about the garden, and blew the chimney-pots down. "This is a delightful spot," he said, "we must ask the Hail on a visit." So the Hail came. Every day for three hours he rattled on the roof of the castle till he broke most of the slates, and then he ran round and round the garden as fast as he could go. He was dressed in grey, and his breath was like ice.

"I can not understand why the spring is so late in coming," said the Selfish Giant, as he sat at the window and looked out at his cold white garden; "I hope there will be a change in the weather."

But the Spring never came, nor the Summer. The Autumn gave golden fruit to every garden, but to the Giant's garden she gave none. "He is too selfish," she said. So it was always Winter there, and the North Wind, and the Hail, and the Frost, and the Snow danced about through the trees.

Interactive Follow-Up Activities

Questions
1. Why did the children like playing in the Giant's garden? *(It was beautiful and large; it had soft grass; they loved to listen to the birdsong)*.
2. Why was the Giant selfish? *(He would not let the children play in his garden)*.
3. What happened in the Giant's garden after he stopped the children playing there? *(It was always winter; the snow, hail, frost and wind made him very miserable)*.

Getting the message
1. How did the children feel when the Giant came back? *(They had nowhere to play; they were sad and bored)*.
2. If you are a selfish person, what do other people think about you? *(Selfish people are often unpopular; they are not liked)*.

3. I'm going to say some things about the story. Put your thumb up if you agree with them and put your thumb down if you think they're wrong:
   - The children were happy playing in the Giant's garden.
   - The Giant was right to build the wall around his own garden.
   - It was winter all year in the Giant's garden because he was selfish.
   - The Giant ended up being miserable.
   - The Giant should let the children share his garden.

Non-interactive Follow-Up

Summary of the story
   - The children used to play in the Giant's beautiful garden after school.
   - The children were very happy there.
   - One day the Giant returned to his castle.
   - He scared the children away and built a wall around the castle and put up a 'keep out' sign.
   - Spring didn't arrive at the Giant's garden – it was winter all year, with snow and hail and frost and a cold north wind.
   - The Giant was miserable because the weather was so bad.

Reflection
The Giant in the story was a selfish giant: he not only made the children sad but he ended up being miserable himself. It's the same with us – if we are selfish, our friends will stay away and we will be lonely and miserable. So, the lesson is: try not to be selfish – share what you have.

Prayer
Lord God, please help us to be kind to others and share all that we have. Help us not to be selfish and unkind like the Selfish Giant, who ended up being miserable, cold and lonely. Give us hearts to think of others, like Jesus. Amen.

Objective
To help children learn the value of being unselfish.

RE themes
Christianity, beliefs and practice: loving others.

Props
(Not essential): a copy of the book *The Selfish Giant* by Oscar Wilde.

Introduction
Today we're having the second part of the story of the Selfish Giant. If you remember, the children used to play happily in the Giant's beautiful garden but when the Giant returned, he scared them away and built a wall around the garden so that they had nowhere to play. Then it was winter all the time in the garden and the Giant was very miserable.

Story: The Selfish Giant by Oscar Wilde (Part 2)

One morning the Giant was lying awake in bed when he heard some lovely music. It sounded so sweet to his ears that he thought it must be the king's musicians passing by. It was really only a little linnet singing outside his window, but it was so long since he had heard a bird sing in his garden that it seemed to him to be the most beautiful music in the world. Then the Hail stopped dancing over his head, and the North Wind ceased roaring, and a delicious perfume came to him through the open casement. "I believe the Spring has come at last," said the Giant; and he jumped out of bed and looked out.

What did he see?

He saw a most wonderful sight. Through a little hole in the wall the children had crept in, and they were sitting in the branches of the trees. In every tree that he could see there was a little child. And the trees were so glad to have the children back again that they had covered themselves with blossoms, and were waving their arms gently above the children's heads. The birds were flying about and twittering with delight, and the flowers were looking up through the green grass and laughing. It was a lovely scene, only in one corner it was still winter. It was the farthest corner of the garden, and in it was standing a little boy. He was so small that he could not reach up to the branches of the tree, and he was wandering all round it, crying bitterly. The poor tree was still quite covered with frost and snow, and the North Wind was blowing and roaring above it. "Climb up, little boy," said the Tree, and it bent its branches down as low as it could; but the boy was too tiny.

And the Giant's heart melted as he looked out. "How selfish I have been!" he said; "now I know why the Spring would not come here. I will put that poor little boy on the top of the tree, and then I will knock down the wall, and my garden shall be the children's playground for ever and ever." He was really very sorry for what he had done.

So he crept downstairs and opened the front door quite softly, and went out into the garden. But when the children saw him they were so frightened that they all ran away, and the garden became winter again. Only the little boy did not run, for his eyes were so full of tears that he did not see the Giant coming. And the Giant stole up behind him and took him gently in his hand, and put him up into the tree. And the tree broke at once into blossoms, and the birds came and sang on it, and the little boy stretched out his two arms and flung them round the Giant's neck, and kissed him. And the other children, when they saw that the Giant was not wicked any longer, came running back, and with them came the Spring. "It is your garden now, little children," said the Giant, and he took a great axe and knocked down the wall. And when the people were going to market at twelve o'clock they found the Giant playing with the children in the most beautiful garden they had ever seen.

All day long they played, and in the evening they came to the Giant to bid him good-bye.

"But where is your little companion?" he said: "the boy I put into the tree." The Giant loved him the best because he had kissed him.

"We don't know," answered the children; "he has gone away."

"You must tell him to be sure and come here tomorrow," said the Giant. But the children said that they did not know where he lived, and had never seen him before; and the Giant felt very sad.

Every afternoon, when school was over, the children came and played with the Giant. But the little boy whom the Giant loved was never seen again. The Giant was very kind to all the children, yet he longed for his first little friend, and often spoke of him. "How I would like to see him!" he used to say.

Years went over, and the Giant grew very old and feeble. He could not play about any more, so he sat in a huge armchair, and watched the children at their games, and admired his garden. "I have many beautiful flowers," he said; "but the children are the most beautiful flowers of all."

One winter morning he looked out of his window as he was dressing. He did not hate the Winter now, for he knew that it was merely the Spring asleep, and that the flowers were resting.

Suddenly he rubbed his eyes in wonder, and looked and looked. It certainly was a marvellous sight. In the farthest corner of the garden was a tree quite covered with lovely white blossoms. Its branches were all golden, and silver fruit hung down from them, and underneath it stood the little boy he had loved.

Downstairs ran the Giant in great joy, and out into the garden. He hastened across the grass, and came near to the child. And when he came quite close his face grew red with anger, and he said, "Who hath dared to wound thee?" For on the palms of the child's hands were the prints of two nails, and the prints of two nails were on the little feet.

"Who hath dared to wound thee?" cried the Giant, "tell me, that I may take my big sword and slay him."

"Nay!" answered the child; "but these are the wounds of Love."

"Who art thou?" said the Giant, and a strange awe fell on him, and he knelt before the little child.

And the child smiled on the Giant, and said to him, "You let me play once in your garden, today you shall come with me to my garden, which is Paradise."

And when the children ran in that afternoon, they found the Giant lying dead under the tree, all covered with white blossoms.

Interactive Follow-Up Activities

Questions
1. Why did the spring return to the Giant's garden? *(Because the children had crept in through a hole in the wall).*
2. How did the Giant feel about the children being in his garden again? *(He was happy because he realised that's why spring had not returned; he realised he had been selfish).*
3. What happened after the Giant knocked down the wall? *(The children were allowed to play in the garden; the Giant made friends with them; he was not selfish any more).*

Getting the message
1. Why was the Giant angry when he saw the little boy? *(He had been wounded).*
2. Who was the little boy and how do you know? *(It was Jesus; he had nail marks; he said that the old Giant would join him in Paradise, which is Heaven; he mysteriously disappeared).*
3. Call out the right word to finish each of these sentences about the story:
   - The children came back to play in the Giant's _____. *(garden)*
   - The Giant helped the little _____. *(boy)*
   - The Giant knocked down the wall with his _____. *(axe)*
   - The Giant was sorry that he had been very _____. *(selfish)*
   - There were nail marks on the little boy's hands and _____. *(feet)*

Non-interactive Follow-Up

Summary of the story
- Spring returned to the Giant's garden when the children crept in through a hole in the wall.
- There was one little boy who couldn't reach a tree like the others.
- The Giant realised he had been selfish – he helped the little boy into the tree and received a hug and a kiss from him.
- The Giant knocked down the wall and welcomed the children.
- The Giant grew old but the little boy didn't come back.
- One day the little boy returned; he had nail marks on his hands and feet.
- The boy told the Giant he would join him in Paradise; the Giant was found dead the next day.

Reflection
The Giant realised that he had been selfish and he let the children play in his garden again. We are usually much happier when we share our things too, so remember this story and always try to be like the kind Giant and not the selfish Giant.

Prayer
Lord God, thank You that we have wonderful stories like *The Selfish Giant* to teach us important things. Help us to learn from them. Help us to be kind like the Giant was in the end and not selfish like he was at first. Amen.

Objective
To help children understand the work of an important Christian organisation.

RE themes
Christianity, beliefs and practice: loving others, William Booth (Salvation Army).

Props
(Not essential): a picture of a Salvation Army badge.

Introduction
You may have seen a smart-looking brass band playing in a town, especially playing carols near Christmas. If all the musicians were wearing dark uniforms then it was probably a Salvation Army band. But what is the Salvation Army? Here is the story.

Life Story: William Booth

William Booth lived a long time ago, in the days of Queen Victoria. As a teenage boy he worked in a shop where poor people would sell their belongings for a few pennies. He saw what miserable lives many of these people led and often wondered what he could do to help them.

William was a Christian who went to church each week and dreamt of becoming a preacher: he wanted to stand at the front of a church and tell people how good God was and how they should help others. Later on, William did become a preacher working in a church, but he often wondered why the poor people he so wanted to help didn't come along.

One day William went outside and found some homeless men on the streets dressed in rags, and took them into his church. The people in the church complained and told the men to sit at the back because they were dirty and smelly. William realised why these poor people didn't come to church – they were simply not welcome.

William talked to his wife about the problem. They decided the only thing to do was to leave the church and go out into the street where the poor people were. They left their home in Nottingham and moved to London. Walking round the busy streets, William was shocked to see how many people needed help: there were poor people, homeless people, drunks, sick people, disabled people and children who had nowhere to go. He knew that he needed to help them and he knew that they needed to know God.

William bought a large tent and held a special meeting called a mission. There was a soup kitchen and volunteers came to help the sick and the elderly. At first, people were suspicious but when they found out that William and his helpers were kind and friendly, word soon got around. William persuaded wealthy Christians to give him money so that he could buy food for the hungry. But William wanted more: he wanted to buy places for homeless people to sleep in, and safe homes for women and children.

After years of preaching and helping others and working tirelessly, William Booth had built a whole organisation of Christians who helped the poor people of London. They had buildings and soup kitchens and safe houses. Thousands of people became Christians and started to live better lives. William said that fighting poverty was like a battle and so his people were like soldiers. They became known as The Salvation Army and that is what they are known as today, about 150 years after William Booth went out onto the streets.

The Salvation Army was given lots of money by people who could see how much good they were doing. They began to work in other towns and cities and then even in other countries. Today, the Salvation Army helps needy people all over the world. How big is it? Well it has:

- Over 500 shelters for homeless people
- Hundreds of homes for children, elderly and disabled people
- Hundreds of homes for other people who need help or somewhere safe to go
- Over one million members who give their time to look after people in need.

The Salvation Army also runs nurseries, health centres, emergency food centres, cafes, kitchens and hostels. Its volunteers visit thousands of prisoners each year and give advice to anyone who needs it. All this started with one man, who cared and who knew that God would help him.

Interactive Follow-Up Activities

Questions
1. Why didn't homeless people go to William's church? *(They didn't feel welcome; people said they were dirty and smelly)*.
2. Why did William go to London? *(To help poor people on the streets; to take the church to them)*.
3. What sort of things does the Salvation Army do today? *(Feeds people, provides homes, gives help and advice, etc.)*.

Getting the message
1. Who did William help on the streets of London? *(The poor, homeless, needy, hungry, lost, old, young, vulnerable, sick and disabled)*.
2. Why is it difficult to help people on the streets? *(They are often suspicious of strangers, it is dangerous, it can be cold, dirty and dark)*.

3. Let's see what you know about the Salvation Army. Put your thumbs up for true things I say and put your thumbs down for false things:
   - They help homeless people. *(T)*
   - They provide homes and shelters for street children around the world. *(T)*
   - They are Christians. *(T)*
   - They only work in London. *(F)*
   - Their money comes from donations given by people. *(T)*
   - They dress up like soldiers. *(T)*

Non-interactive Follow-Up

Summary of the story
- William Booth lived in the time of Queen Victoria.
- He wanted to help the poor from an early age when he worked in a shop.
- He became a preacher, which was his ambition.
- He found that most churchgoers didn't want poor people in the church.
- William moved to London and started a street mission helping needy people.
- He started a Christian organisation called The Salvation Army.
- With lots of donations, The Salvation Army spread all over the world and provides homes and lots of different kinds of help for thousands of people who are in need.

Reflection
William Booth was a wonderful man because he was always thinking of other people and how he could help them. Remember to think of ways in which you can help someone else, even if it is just by saying a kind word.

Prayer
Lord God, thank You for The Salvation Army and for the courage and kindness of William Booth who founded it. Thank You that there are men and women all around the world who give their time to help the poor and the sick and the homeless, just like Jesus taught us to do. Amen.

Objective
To help children understand how Christians apply their faith to their occupations and lifestyle.

RE themes
Christianity, belief and practice.

Props
A football.
A photo of Kaka (playing football in the yellow top of Brazil, ideally).

Introduction
Who likes football?
Here is a true story about a man who is one of the best footballers in the world. He is also a Christian and this assembly is about his life and how his Christian faith helps him.

Kaka: footballer of faith

Kaka is the name of one of the best footballers in the world. He is from Brazil and he plays for AC Milan, one of the most famous teams in Italy. In 2002 Kaka helped to win the World Cup playing for Brazil and in 2007 he was voted the best player in the world.

But things could have been very different for Kaka. When he was 18 years old he went to see his grandfather. Kaka always loved going there and one reason was that his grandfather had a small swimming pool in his back garden. Kaka loved swimming and he also loved sliding down the water slide.

But one day, at the pool, there was a nasty accident. Kaka went down the water slide but fell as he slid and he dropped into the water head first. Kaka hit his head against the bottom of the pool. It was very painful and he could tell that he had hurt himself.

After lying down for a while Kaka had to get back to his football club to do training for the next match. But when he got there, the other players could tell that he was not well. The club manager sent him to the hospital so he could be checked out. At the hospital doctors examined Kaka and asked him about the accident at the swimming pool.

Kaka had an x-ray which showed that one of the bones in his neck was cracked. "This is serious," said the doctor. "You will have to stop playing football for a long time. You'll have to wear a neck brace. You were lucky – it could have been a lot worse."

Kaka was sad that he couldn't play football: it was his job and he loved the game. But Kaka was determined to get better right away. He prayed to God that his broken neck would be healed quickly. Kaka is a Christian and his faith in God helped him to get through this difficult time. He kept on praying.

After just two months his neck felt better. He tried playing football and it didn't hurt. Kaka was overjoyed and so were his team-mates – after all, Kaka was one of the best players in the world! He thanked God for his recovery and felt sure that God answered his prayers.

Today, Kaka plays his football in Italy. Every time he scores a goal he points up to heaven and gives thanks to God. His Christian faith is very important to him and he likes to tell people about it. In 2002 when Brazil won the World Cup, Kaka took off his yellow jersey to show a T-shirt underneath with a message written on it. "I belong to Jesus" it said.

Kaka reads the Bible as part of his belief. "I want to live my life in the right way, close to God," he says. "Reading the Bible and praying were the things that got me through those difficult times."

Kaka doesn't just pray and read the Bible. He tries to help other people, like Jesus taught. He gives away a lot of his money to help people who are in need. He is also a supporter of the World Food Programme, which takes emergency food to the places where people are really starving and suffering.

Kaka is famous but it is faith that matters to him most, not fame.

Interactive Follow-Up Activities

Questions
1. What happened to Kaka at the swimming pool? *(He fell into the water and hit his head on the bottom of the pool).*
2. What did Kaka do when the doctors told him that he had a broken neck? *(He prayed that God would heal him).*
3. Why is reading the Bible important to Kaka? *(Because it guides him on how to live his life).*

Getting the message
1. Kaka is famous but he helps others – why do you think he does this? *(He believes in Jesus who taught that we should help others).*
2. Why do you think Kaka thanks God when he scores a goal? *(Because he believes God healed him when he broke his neck).*
3. A role-model is someone who you can look up to and try to copy in the way they behave and live their life. Do you think that Kaka has been a good role model for Christians in sport? Why do you think that? *(Yes, because he has always been open about his faith and has publically thanked God for his healing and success).*

4. When you lose a game you've been playing, do you:
   - get cross
   - say you don't care
   - say to yourself you'll win next time
   - congratulate the person who wins.

   Which do you think is the best reaction?

Non-interactive Follow-Up

Summary of the story
- Kaka is one of the best footballers in the world and plays for Brazil.
- When he was 18 he had an accident in a swimming pool and broke his neck.
- A doctor told him he would be out of football for a long time.
- As a Christian he prayed to God. His neck was better after just two months.
- Kaka reads the Bible and prays so he can live the way he believes God wants him to.
- He helps other people by giving money to food programmes and charity work.

Reflection
Kaka has used his talent and gifts to tell other people about God and is thankful that he is well enough to play football. Even though he is rich and famous he tries to help other people who are in need, which is a good thing to do.

Prayer
Lord God, thank You for Kaka, for his great gifts as a footballer and for the pleasure he has given to so many people. Help us to learn from his example and follow You in everything we think, say and do. Amen.

12 Mary Jones and her Bible

Objective
To help children understand the relevance and importance of the Bible to Christians.

RE themes
Christianity, beliefs and practice, The Bible.

Props
Any of: a Bible (a large King James version if possible).
A large map/posters/pictures of Wales and Welsh mountains (to show distance and terrain).
A pair of old-fashioned black boots.
Bible Society publicity material.

Introduction
Can you imagine walking 25 miles on your own in big uncomfortable boots and eventually bare feet across mountains, rivers and fields? This is the true story of one little girl, not that much older than you, who did just that because she desperately wanted a Bible....

True Story: Mary Jones and her Bible

Once, a long time ago, a young girl called Mary Jones lived in a very small village in the Welsh mountains. Mary was a very kind and helpful child who always saw the best in every situation and in every person. Everybody loved her.

Mary went to the small village school and enjoyed her lessons enormously. She particularly enjoyed RE and learning about the Bible, although she had never seen one. Her teacher told the children stories from the Bible but it was a very poor village and school and so there were only a very few books and pictures. Every book they had was very special to them all.

One day a travelling preacher came to the village school and he talked to the children about the Bible and told them many stories. But the most amazing thing for Mary was that the preacher actually owned a Bible, which he showed to the children. He told them that very few Bibles were printed, but every so often he received a few which he was able to sell to people. Mary was really desperate to own her own Bible and she asked the preacher how she might manage to do that. The preacher told her how much the Bible would cost and when he was likely to get some to sell. From that moment, Mary was absolutely determined to have her own Bible and she decided to do any odd jobs she could for any person in the village so that she could save up to buy one. She fed people's chickens, cleaned them out, ran errands, sewed and mended, cooked, cleaned, washed and dried clothes, looked after children, baked and did everything she could to earn money. She saved and saved and after a whole year, she had managed to save enough.

Mary knew when the preacher was going to get some new copies of the Bible and planned her journey to meet him. The preacher lived 25 miles away and the only way Mary could get there was to walk. So she walked and walked – through muddy fields, across streams, up and down mountainsides, through woodland, past several small villages and eventually her feet hurt so much she had to take off her boots and walk barefoot.

When she finally arrived at the preacher's house, she was exhausted and fell into his arms when he opened the door. The preacher was speechless when he saw Mary and amazed when he realised how long she had saved, how hard she had worked and how far she had travelled to buy the Bible she so desperately wanted. But, the preacher was also very troubled as he had no more Bibles left – the one he had was saved for someone else who had bought it. He had to tell Mary that, even though she had worked so hard and travelled so far, there was no Bible for her.

Mary set off home again broken-hearted, but refused to give up. She was going to get her own Bible one day!

When she had gone, the preacher thought that he just had to do something to help her. So, he hurried to see the person who had asked him to save the last Bible for them. Imagine how pleased he was when that kind person agreed to let Mary have the Bible! The preacher managed to catch up with Mary who was overjoyed when she at last held her very own Bible.

When Mary grew up she didn't want other people to have to struggle to own a Bible in the way she had, and so she started an organisation called The Bible Society which today provides copies of the Bible anywhere in the world for everybody who wants one.

Interactive Follow-Up Activities

Questions
1. Where did Mary Jones live? *(In a small village in the Welsh mountains).*
2. What did Mary particularly enjoy at school? *(RE lessons and stories from the Bible).*
3. Was there a Bible and lots of books like we have in Mary's school? *(No, but all the books were cherished and loved because there were so few).*

Getting the message
1. What happened at the school to make Mary really want to own her own Bible? *(A visiting preacher came to the school and she saw a Bible for the first time. The preacher told her that he sometimes received Bibles that he was able to sell).*

2. What kind of jobs did Mary do to save up enough money to buy her Bible? *(She fed people's chickens, cleaned them out, ran errands, sewed and mended, cooked, cleaned, washed and dried clothes, looked after children, baked and did absolutely everything she could to earn money)*.
3. Is there anything that you would work that hard for? Why?
4. Put your hand up if...
   - You would work for a year doing sometimes horrible jobs to save up for something that really mattered to you.
   - You would walk 25 miles through mud, mountains and fields to buy a Bible.
   - You would rather wait for a bookshop to open in your village to buy a Bible.
   - You enjoy listening to stories from the Bible.

Non-interactive Follow-Up

Summary of the story
- Mary Jones lived in a small village in the Welsh mountains.
- She loved listening to Bible stories and became determined to have her own to read after she had seen one belonging to a visiting preacher.
- She saved and worked for over a year before she could afford to buy one.
- She walked on her own for 25 miles over difficult countryside to reach the village where she could buy her Bible.
- When she grew up she set up the Bible Society, which provides Bibles internationally for those that want one.

Reflection
Mary Jones knew how important it is for Christians to read the Bible. She also knew that in order to have something you want, the best way is to work hard and to save. If we have a lot of things, we shouldn't take them for granted. Try and remember to be grateful for everything you have and to thank the people that look after you.

Prayer
Lord God, thank You for Mary Jones and for the example she gave us. Help us to work hard and to give thanks to You and to the people that care for us. Amen.

13 | The Old Watch

Objective
To help children learn about the value of forgiveness.

RE themes
Christianity, beliefs and practice, parables, forgiveness.

Props
(Not essential): an old pocket watch on a chain, or a picture of one.

Introduction
Today's story is all about a beautiful old watch. It's based on a story in the Bible that Jesus once told: listen carefully....

Story: The Old Watch

Emil loved staying with his Gran and Grandad. For a start, they lived in North Wales, near the sea and near some fantastic big mountains. They had a wonderful garden full of fruit and vegetables, which Emil was allowed to pick, and you could see Conway Castle from their kitchen window. It was a great place to spend a few days in the summer, especially as Emil's annoying little sister Penny stayed at home.

The best thing about staying at Gran and Grandad's, though, was the glass cabinet in the living room. It was full of really interesting old treasures which they had collected over the years. There was a pot of old coins from all around the world, including a gold one from China; a beautiful little carved wooden owl; a brass magnifying glass in a leather case and a real tiger's claw, which Grandad brought back from India. There were other things too, but Emil's favourite object was the silver pocket watch.

It wasn't the kind of watch that you wear on your wrist: it had no strap, but instead hung from a long metal chain. It was round and very large and heavy too, with strange curvy writing on the back which Emil had never been able to read. The front had a glass lid which you could open, and the hands were delicate and fancy. There was a winder on top – Grandad showed Emil how to wind the watch up: you had to do it very carefully because there was a special spring inside which could break – old watches like this don't have batteries.

Emil never got bored with holding the watch and wondering who had owned it in the past. Grandad said it was made of real silver and was over a hundred years old. Emil loved to hear its gentle tick and watch the fragile hands passing across the Roman numerals on the face. Emil was allowed to open the glass case to get the watch out by himself now that he was seven years old, and that's just what he did one Sunday morning while Grandad was in the garden and Gran was busy in the kitchen.

Emil took out the watch and wound it up. He then pretended to be a fine gentleman, telling the time to a passer-by. After this, Emil held the watch by its long chain and swung it gently back and forth. He'd heard on TV that you could hypnotise someone by doing that. He wasn't sure what hypnotise meant but he decided to give it a try. He swung the watch back and forward, staring at the hands until his eyes hurt. He pretended that he had become a hypnotised monster. He jumped up and started to growl. Then he swung the watch around his head as if he was going to hurl it miles away.

And then a terrible thing happened. Emil didn't mean to let go of the watch, but it happened. As he was swinging it quickly and being the scary monster, the chain just slipped out of his hand. The silver pocket watch flew across the room and landed with a sharp crack in the fireplace. Emil froze. He looked at the door and the window. No one had seen him. He ran over to the fireplace and picked up the watch. The glass was smashed and one of the delicate silver hands was broken. Emil began to cry.

It was Gran that heard him first. She hurried into the room and asked him what was the matter. With tears flowing from his eyes, Emil held out the broken watch and said nothing. His chest was throbbing and he needed a tissue.

"Come on, we'd better show your Grandad," said Gran.

Grandad was not pleased. He looked at the watch and pulled a stern face.

"It's going to cost a lot of money to get this fixed Emil."

"I'm really really sorry," sobbed Emil. "It was an accident."

"Don't worry, I'm sure it was. And I don't suppose you've got lots of money to give me to get it fixed, have you, Emil?"

Emil shook his head. He didn't have any money at all.

"Well, there's only one thing to do. We'll forgive you, and we'll pay to get it fixed." Grandad rubbed Emil's hair the way he usually did. Emil suddenly felt much better.

The next day, Emil's mum and dad came to collect him. They talked with Grandad and Gran about the broken watch for ages. He was quite glad to be back home, where he could forget all about the accident. While he was unpacking his suitcase in his bedroom, Emil's sister Penny wandered in, with mum behind her. She had her hands behind her back.

"Go on, Penny," said mum.

"Er Emil, I need to show you something," said Penny. She brought her hands forward and showed Emil a small toy car. It had broken wheels and was scratched. "I'm very sorry Emil, but you left it outside the back door and I trod on it by accident. The wheels are bent."

Emil suddenly screeched with anger.

"That was one of my best toys. How could you? It's ruined." He looked at mum. "She'll have to buy me a new one now." Then Penny began to cry.

"But I haven't got enough money."

"You still have to get me a new toy," said Emil.

Then mum stepped in. She put an arm around Penny and gave Emil a sharp look. "Right, I need to have a word with you, young man." And she did.

Interactive Follow-Up Activities

Questions
1. How did the silver pocket watch get broken? *(Emil was playing with it and pretending to be a monster; it was an accident).*
2. Why did Emil like the watch so much? *(It was old and interesting; it was valuable and unusual).*
3. Why did Grandad forgive Emil for breaking the watch? *(He knew that Emil didn't break it on purpose; Emil could not afford to get it fixed; he was young; there was no point in making him feel guilty).*

Getting the message
1. How did Emil react when his sister broke his car? *(He was angry and unforgiving).*
2. How should he have reacted? *(He should have forgiven her because he was forgiven over the watch).*
3. What would you have said to Emil at the end if you were his mum?
4. The story of the old watch was all about forgiveness. Jesus taught that we should forgive people when they do something wrong to us – this means we should let them off and not try to do anything bad to them. Put your hand up if you think people should be forgiven for doing these things:
   - For bumping into you accidentally in the playground.
   - For laughing at you when you fall over.
   - For making your shoes dirty.
   - For breaking your pencil.
   - For saying nasty words to you.

Non-interactive Follow-Up

Summary of the story

- Emil liked staying with his Gran and Grandad in North Wales.
- He loved looking at his Grandad's old silver pocket watch.
- The watch was old and valuable.
- Emil accidentally broke the watch when he was playing with it.
- Emil's Gran and Grandad forgave him, even though it would cost a lot to fix.
- Emil went home and his sister told him she had broken one of his toy cars by accident.
- Emil was very cross and did not want to forgive her.

Reflection

We all make mistakes from time to time. We all have accidents and we all hurt people sometimes whether we mean to or not. We must learn that if we want to be forgiven when we go wrong, then we must forgive people who hurt us.

Prayer

Lord God, help us to forgive people who hurt us in different ways. Help us to understand that we must forgive other people if we want them to forgive us when we do bad things. Thank You for the lessons that Jesus taught us about this. Amen.

14 Carlo's Christmas Card

Objective
To help children understand the importance of helping others.

RE themes
Christianity, beliefs and practice, parables, helping others.

Props
(Not essential): a small Christmas card.

Introduction
Today's story is about a girl, a boy and a Christmas card.

Story: Carlo's Christmas Card

"Stop it, that hurt!" Michelle looked across the playground to see who was shouting. It was her friend Ashia: she was lying on her back and rubbing her elbow. Carlo was standing next to her. He must have pushed her over – Carlo was always pushing people over in the playground. Michelle didn't like him at all. He had caused lots of trouble at school since he had joined the class just three weeks ago. Michelle walked over and helped her friend get to her feet.

"Are you alright Ashia?"

"I've got mud on my coat and my elbow stings," said Ashia. "I didn't do anything to Carlo – he just said I was annoying him then he pushed me over."

"Never mind," said Michelle. "We'll tell Mrs Jones what he did. I'll ask her if you can help me give out the Christmas cards after play as well – it's my turn today."

Mrs Jones, Michelle and Ashia's teacher, agreed to let the girls sort out the Christmas cards for their class that had been posted in the school's special letterbox. It was very exciting, especially as there were only two weeks left before Christmas. There was a huge pile of envelopes to give out in the class and the two girls walked around, handing them to their classmates. At the end Michelle had six to open and Ashia had four.

"Did everyone get a card?" said Ashia.

"I don't think Carlo got one," said Michelle.

"Well I'm not surprised," said Ashia, "the way he treats people."

Michelle glanced across towards Carlo. Ashia was right, he was the only child in the class who wasn't opening a card. He looked very miserable.

The following Sunday, Michelle was in Sunday school at church. Mr Besitas, the teacher, was talking about helping other people at Christmas.

"It's lovely to receive presents at Christmas isn't it? I'm sure that you're all going to be given lots of lovely things on December 25 and I'm sure I will too. In my family we try not to spend too much money on each other, though – we buy presents for one another but not great big expensive ones. For a start, we don't really need lots of big expensive things and also, we like to help people who maybe won't be having such a nice Christmas."

Michelle listened carefully as Mr Besitas explained how his family always gave a donation of money to The Salvation Army at Christmas, so that homeless people could have a small present and also share in a proper hot Christmas dinner at one of the shelters in town.

"We try to follow what Jesus taught us to do," he said. "Jesus said that we should help others, and not just our friends, but also strangers." Everyone nodded that it was the right thing to do. "Jesus said that we should even help people that we don't like," added Mr Besitas. "So, this Christmas, think what you can do to help someone – even if it's just a very small kindness."

All the way home, Michelle kept thinking about what Mr Besitas had said. And she kept thinking about Carlo. She really didn't like him, it was true, but she remembered how sad he had looked in the classroom on Friday. "I would hate to be the only person who didn't get a Christmas card," she said to herself.

When Michelle got home, she asked her mum if she had any spare Christmas cards.

"I thought you had some left," said mum. "I bought you a whole box of Disney ones remember."

"Yes, but have you got any really nice ones? I mean, the Disney ones are nice, but is there a bigger one somewhere?" Mum gave Michelle a questioning look then went over to a drawer in the living room.

"There are a couple of those ones with golden stars on left."

"Ooh yes – can I have one?" said Michelle.

"OK," said mum. "Who's it for: Mrs Jones?"

"Er, no," said Michelle. "It's for... a friend."

Interactive Follow-Up Activities

Questions
1. Who was the Christmas card for? *(It was for Carlo)*.
2. Why was Michelle going to give Carlo a card even though she didn't like him? *(Because she felt sorry for him; because she wanted to follow Jesus' teaching about helping others, even people you don't like)*.
3. Why do you think Carlo didn't get any cards? *(He was unpopular because he kept pushing people; he was new to the school; he may have been lonely)*.

Getting the message

1. What did Mr Besitas do at Christmas? *(He gave money to the Salvation Army to help homeless people have a present and a meal at Christmas).*
2. What did Jesus teach about helping people? *(It is right to help others, including strangers and people you don't like).*
3. Maybe you've seen someone at school who needs cheering up. Put your hand up if you've ever done one of these:
   - Gone to talk to someone in the playground who looks lonely.
   - Sent a Christmas card to someone who isn't one of your best friends.
   - Shared something with someone who looks upset.
   - Asked to be partners with someone who feels left out.
   - Asked a boy or girl who is new to the school to play with you.

Non-interactive Follow-Up

Summary of the story

- Michelle's friend Ashia was pushed over in the playground by Carlo, a new boy.
- Michelle and Ashia gave out the class Christmas cards after break.
- Carlo was the only person not to receive a card: he looked very sad.
- At Sunday school, Michelle's teacher Mr Besitas talked about helping others at Christmas.
- He said that Jesus taught us to help strangers and even people we don't like.
- Michelle thought about Carlo and felt sorry for him not getting a card.
- She asked her mum for an extra nice card to give Carlo.

Reflection

Nobody likes being left out and lonely when everybody else seems to be having fun. Try to remember to be kind to someone that you don't usually play with over the next week. Be a person who helps others who are left out – you might get left out yourself one day.

Prayer

Lord God, thank You for showing us how to help others, especially those people who are lonely or sad. Please help us to be kind to other people, both at home and at school. Amen.

Objective
To help children understand the importance of helping others.

RE themes
Christianity, beliefs and practice, parables, helping others.

Props
(None).

Introduction
I hope you help out at home. Today's story is about two children who were asked to do just that.

Story: The Helpful Hedgehog

Mrs Hogg was getting worried. Hedgehogs often worry, and Mrs Hogg was a bigger worrier than most. For a start, she was always worried about finding enough food to eat. Secondly, she was worried about badgers, who were always sniffing around her part of the woods. But mainly she worried about her two naughty children, Hebe and Hazel.

Hebe and Hazel never seemed to be around when Mrs Hogg needed them and she needed them right now. The autumn was coming and Mrs Hogg needed to prepare a nest under the old hawthorn bush to hibernate in through the coming winter.

"Hebe! Hazel! Where are you?" They were out playing of course, but why didn't they stay nearby like she told them to? Trouble, nothing but trouble. Mrs Hogg snuffled and scratched her way under the hawthorn bush. It was full of snail shells and stones and spiky twigs. She would need lots of help to get the nest ready – all these bits needed clearing out and lots of nice dry leaves needed collecting. She went in search of the children again.

Mrs Hogg found Hebe first. She was watching a butterfly sunbathing on a tree trunk down by the stream.

"Oh there you are Hebe," said Mrs Hogg. "I've been looking for you all over the woods. Now you know that it's autumn don't you Hebe, and that we need to get the nest ready for winter. Well, I'd like you to help me clear out the stones and twigs, and then collect some leaves please."

"Aww mum, do I have to? I'm really busy here watching the butterflies. You know how much I love watching them and they might fly away soon. This could be my last chance. Why don't you ask Hazel to help you – I do much more than her." Mrs Hogg was not pleased at all, but she was far too busy to get into an argument with Hebe, so she went off in search of Hazel.

Mrs Hogg found Hazel looking for worms at the edge of Farmer Plum's barley field.

"Oh there you are Hazel," said Mrs Hogg. "I've been looking for you all over the woods. Now you know that it's autumn don't you Hazel, and that we need to get the nest ready for winter. Well, I'd like you to help me clear out the stones and twigs, and then collect some leaves please."

"OK, mum," said Hazel with a smile. "I'll be along in two ticks. I just want to catch a couple of worms first – I'm really hungry after playing chase the centipede all morning." "Alright dear," said Mrs Hogg, feeling pleased. "Good girl. I'll see you down at the nest in a few minutes." And off she scurried.

Back at the nest, Mrs Hogg got to work while she waited for Hazel to come and help. She cleared out sixteen snail shells and twenty-eight stones, and was just about to start on the prickly twigs when she realised that Hazel hadn't turned up yet. "That's odd," said Mrs Hogg. "She said she'd come and help, but half an hour has passed and there's no sign of her. Well, she'll be along in a minute I suppose." Just then, Mrs Hogg heard the snuffling, hurrying sound of a small hedgehog approaching the nest. But it wasn't Hazel it was Hebe! And she was carrying a big pile of dried leaves.

"Hi mum," said Hebe.

"Well, that's strange," said Mrs Hogg – "I really expected it to be Hazel. I thought you weren't going to help."

"I know," said Hebe. "But while I was watching the butterflies, I thought about you doing all the work and decided it wasn't fair. So I thought I'd come and help after all. Now, shall I clear out the prickly twigs?"

"Oh, right, er, yes please dear."

With Hebe's help, Mrs Hogg cleared out the nest in no time, and filled it with lovely soft leaves. Just when they were finished, Hazel arrived.

She saw that all the work had been done. "Oh sorry, mum, I forgot all about helping you – I got quite carried away catching worms."

"Oh well," said Mrs Hogg looking at Hebe. "It's done now, so never mind."

Interactive Follow-Up Activities

Questions
1. What did Mrs Hogg need help with? *(Clearing out her nest for hibernation)*.
2. What did Hebe and Hazel say when Mrs Hogg asked them to help? *(Hebe didn't want to help but Hazel said she would)*.
3. What happened in the end? *(Hebe came back to help Mrs Hogg but Hazel forgot)*.

Getting the message

1. Which hedgehog was the most helpful? *(Hebe, because Hazel didn't help at all).*
2. What can we learn from this story? *(You should always do what you say you're going to do; actions speak louder than words; help at home!)*
3. Here's a list. Nod your head if you agree with these things and shake your head sensibly if you don't agree.
   - It's good to help out at home.
   - You should always do what you say you're going to do.
   - It's OK not to keep promises.
   - It's all right to let your parents down.
   - If you forget to do something you should say sorry.

Non-interactive Follow-Up

Summary of the story
- Mrs Hogg the hedgehog needed help with getting her nest ready for hibernation.
- She looked for her two children, Hebe and Hazel to ask them for help.
- Hebe didn't want to help because she was busy watching butterflies.
- Hazel said she would help.
- Mrs Hogg started doing the work but Hazel didn't come to help.
- Hebe turned up to help after changing her mind.
- Mrs Hogg was not too pleased with Hazel.

Reflection
It's very important if you tell someone you're going to do something, that you actually do it. If you forget or let people down then people will think you can't be trusted. Remember, do as you say.

Prayer
Lord God, help us to be helpful at home, even when it doesn't suit us. Help us to keep our word, to do what we say we're going to do. Help us to be trustworthy. Amen.

Objective
To help children understand how people show they belong and what is special about belonging.

RE themes
Christianity, beliefs and practice, parables, helping others.

Props
Pictures showing:

The ichthys acrostic as below:

OHT showing ichthys acrostic:

Iesous	**Jesus**
Christos	**Christ**
Theou	**God's**
Yios	**Son**
Soter	**Saviour**

Introduction
We can't really imagine what it might feel like to be in danger if we say something that someone else doesn't agree with. The first Christians knew. This is how they managed to stay a bit safer....

The Story of the Sign of the Fish

When Jesus was on earth, many people followed Him and listened to Him when He talked. They saw His miracles and were amazed at the wise things He said; they believed that He was who He said He was – the Son of God. They had actually watched Him do things like bring people back to life, heal people of blindness, make people walk again and turn water into wine. They felt He had changed their lives completely and they wanted to live their lives in the way He told them was right. He told them to love one another, be kind to their enemies and not think that things were more important than people.

Christians believe that after Jesus died He came back to life or was resurrected. After lots of people had seen Him and even talked to Him when He'd come back to life, He then went up, or ascended, to Heaven. The people who lived in the same time as Jesus saw all these things happen so, naturally, they were very excited! Those that believed wanted to follow His teachings and tell other people about Him, because Jesus also told them that when they died they too would go to Heaven to be with Him.

Now, although there were many people who were Christians, there were also many people who were not. These people were mainly Romans who were in charge of the area, and other Jews who belonged there – they thought that Jesus was a liar and a dangerous person. Some of these people got very angry about the Christians and wanted to put them in prison, or even worse, kill them. So, it became very dangerous to be known as a Christian.

Sometimes when two strangers met, they thought they might both be Christians but they couldn't ask directly because that would be too dangerous. So one of them might draw the upper half of the fish symbol on the ground like this:

If the other person recognised the symbol, they would add the other half of the sign:

Then they would both know that the other was a believer. If the person didn't recognise the sign it could be rubbed out very quickly, just as it could be drawn very quickly as it is so simple. The sign needed to be simple so that possible enemies wouldn't realise what it meant.

Another name for the sign is *ichthys,* which is the Greek word for fish. Each of the first letters of this word represents the Christian message:

Iesous	**Jesus**
Christos	**Christ**
Theou	**God's**
Yios	**Son**
Soter	**Saviour**

Christians have been using the sign of the fish for a very long time – nearly 2,000 years! It is still used today – so if you see that sign on a car, or perhaps someone wearing a brooch, it means that the person is showing others that they belong to the Christian faith.

© Badger Learning

Interactive Follow-Up Activities

Questions

1. What is a miracle? *(A marvellous event that is supernatural, not something humans can do)*.
2. Why do you think people could easily draw pictures in the ground 2,000 years ago? *(Because there were no proper roads, just sand or dirt tracks)*.
3. What did strangers do if they met another person they thought might be a Christian? *(They drew half of the fish symbol on the ground and waited to see if the person drew the other half)*.

Getting the message

1. Why was it dangerous to be known as a Christian in those early times? *(Because some people thought that Jesus was a liar and did not want people to follow Him. The Christians were in danger of being killed)*.
2. Why did the early Christians choose the sign of the fish to draw as a symbol? *(Because it was very simple, just two strokes, and could be drawn and erased very quickly)*.
3. Put your hand up if...
   - You think you would continue to follow something you think is true even though it might be dangerous.
   - You would draw a sign to show someone you believed in something, even if the other person might not believe the same as you and could put your life in danger.
   - You think that the early Christians were brave people.
   - You think the fish sign was a good one to choose.

Non-interactive Follow-Up

Summary of the story

- Many people followed Jesus after His resurrection and ascension.
- The Romans and Jews persecuted Christians.
- Christians developed a way of communicating with each other by using a secret symbol.
- They drew half of a fish on the ground and waited to see if people drew the other half, which would signify that they were Christians too.
- Christians today still use the fish symbol as a sign that they belong to the Christian faith.

Reflection

Christians nearly 2,000 years ago were prepared to die for their beliefs. They lived as Jesus told them to and found ways of showing that they belonged to the Christian faith in the face of great danger. They have given Christians today an example to follow in being brave and being prepared to speak out for what they believe in.

Prayer

Lord God, thank You for the example of Christians of long ago. Help us to be brave too and to stand up for our beliefs. Amen.

17 A Trip to Romania

Objective
To help children understand the type of work that Christian organisations carry out currently.

RE themes
Christianity, beliefs and practice, helping others.

Props
(Not essential): a map showing the location of Romania.

Introduction
Christians come in all shapes and sizes and do all sorts of things. But they all try to do the things that Jesus told people to do. One of the things that Jesus taught about was helping the poor. Here is the story of someone who did just that.

True Story: A Trip to Romania

Matt was eighteen years old. He had just left school and hadn't yet got a job. He was still wondering what to do with his life. But he knew one thing: he wanted to do some travelling first – he wanted to see some of the world.

Matt was a Christian who belonged to a church in his local town. One day he saw a poster on the noticeboard. It said 'A trip to Romania!' Matt went over and read the details. It said that a man called Dave was taking a minibus to a country called Romania later that summer. There were several young people going and Dave wanted some people from the church to help look after them. Matt liked the sound of the trip and rang Dave to find out more.

Dave was really pleased that Matt was interested in the trip. He explained that he worked with teenagers in the town and every year he drove a group of them to Romania to work with poor children for two weeks. They took along food and toys and other things that the children didn't have. "It sounds great," said Matt. "Put my name down to come along."

Matt thought that he'd better find out something about Romania. He looked in an atlas and an encyclopedia at home. He discovered that it is a large country in the east of Europe, next to the Black Sea. The books said that, although it has many big towns and modern cities, many people living in the countryside, especially, are quite poor compared with people in Britain.

Matt started to collect some things to take for the children. He asked his family and friends to help out and soon he had a large box full of gifts. There were bars of chocolate and packets of sweets, toy cars, picture books, felt pens, drawing paper, dolls, a small football, several pairs of shoes, some t-shirts, coats, and lots of pairs of socks. Matt hoped there was room on the minibus for everything.

After a few more weeks, the day finally came when it was time to go. Matt set off in the big white minibus, along with ten young people from the town and another older volunteer called Anna. There was a huge roof rack on top of the bus piled high with suitcases and plastic boxes to take to Romania. The journey across Europe took three long days but eventually Matt saw signs saying Romania in many different languages.

The minibus drove through towns, past cities and across some big mountains and into the countryside to a remote village. "This is it," said Dave. Everyone was relieved that the long journey was over. The following day, after everyone had rested, the group went to visit the local orphanage. Dave explained that this was a home for children whose parents weren't able to look after them.

Matt was shocked at how poor and shabby the place was. Everything in the small building seemed old and dirty. Many of the children were lying on beds, staring at the ceiling. The place smelled strongly of disinfectant too. Many of the younger children were really excited that they had visitors, however, and the people who worked in the orphanage were very pleased to see Dave again. Matt said 'hello' to some of the older children who had learnt a little bit of English. They were shy at first but soon started to smile at Matt and the other visitors.

The next day the children were given some of the presents that had been brought over from Britain. There was huge excitement among the children. Matt couldn't help noticing how thin and poorly many of them looked as they reached out to take the chocolate and other gifts. "What they really need is people who can look after them properly," said Dave. "And they need a better home than this drab building." Matt agreed – there was so much that could be done to make the children's lives better.

That night, Dave, Matt and Anna got together to pray. Their church had agreed to give some money towards sending some Christians over to Romania to live there and give some proper full-time help to the orphan children. The money wasn't enough to support the project and so they prayed that more would be found. Matt felt that this was something really important and something he'd like to do himself.

The following year, Matt went back to Romania to the same village, but this time to live there and work with the orphans for a whole year. A rich church in America had given thousands of pounds to help set up a project to help the poor children of this area. It was enough money for Matt and four other Christians to live there and to make the orphanage a much better place. In the end, Matt stayed in Romania for much longer. After lots of hard work and gifts of money and prayer, a new home was built for the children: clean and bright and full of toys, and run by trained caring helpers. Matt's trip to Romania had been even more special than he had thought it would be.

Interactive Follow-Up Activities

Questions

1. How did Matt find out about the trip to Romania? *(He saw a noticeboard in church; he called Dave the leader).*
2. What is Romania like? *(It is a big country in eastern Europe, it has modern cities and towns but there are more poor people there than in UK).*
3. Why did Matt decide to live in Romania? *(He wanted to help the children in the orphanage; he knew that people needed to live there to give proper help).*

Getting the message

1. Why did Matt's church and other Christians give money and gifts for this trip? *(Christians follow the teachings of Jesus who said that we should all help the poor and anyone who is in need).*
2. Why did the children need help from other people? *(They could not look after themselves; they had no parents; the area was poor; the orphanage was dirty and scruffy; the children needed help and love from caring volunteers and nurses).*
3. Matt gave his time to help poor children in Romania. What else do Christians do to help poor people? Here's a list – repeat each thing after me:
   - Give money
   - Give food
   - Give presents
   - Pray
   - Visit people
   - Write letters to people who can help
   - Fundraising.

Non-interactive Follow-Up

Summary of the story

- Matt heard about a trip to Romania organised by his church.
- He decided to go along because he wanted to travel.
- He collected gifts and food for the poor children they were going to visit.
- Dave drove Matt and some young people to Romania in a minibus.
- Matt visited the orphanage and noticed how dirty and scruffy it was.
- The children were thin and poorly but were pleased with the gifts.
- After prayer, Matt decided to live in Romania to help the orphans full-time, funded by Christians from around the world.

Reflection

Remember that there are many people around the world, including children, who live in poor conditions. Some have no home, some have no food, some have no one to look after them. Even if we can't all be like Matt, we can all give a little money to charities to help these people.

Prayer

Lord God, thank You that You love and care for the poor all over the world. Thank You that You helped Matt and other Christians to build a new home for those children in Romania. Please help other people who are helping the poor and show us what we can all do. Amen.

Objective

To help children understand how beliefs and actions put into practice can impact the lives of people both nationally and internationally.

RE themes

Christianity, beliefs and practice, helping others.

Props

Fair Trade logo.
Examples of Fair Trade merchandise, e.g. tea, coffee, chocolate and bananas.
Pictures of farmers and Fair Trade groups available from www.fairtrade.org.uk.
Globe to show where different foods come from.
Cards for children to read out as fair-trade growers and those who don't belong to fair-trade (see below).
Visualiser for Interactive Follow-Up Activities (not essential).

Introduction

Do you go to the supermarket with your family? There are so many things to choose from, aren't there? When we go, we have to make choices about absolutely everything – such as baked beans, cereals, chocolate and bananas. This assembly is about a choice that you could talk about with your mums and dads the next time you go shopping....

Fair Trade: A True Story

What is your favourite cereal? Are you allowed to choose whatever you like, or maybe you're only allowed things like porridge or bran flakes? What about chocolate – do you have one day in the week when you're allowed sweets or do you have them whenever you ask? Different families have different rules – but whatever we choose, we don't often think about the people that actually grow or make the things we eat.

Much of the food we eat and buy in the shops comes from other countries: tea and coffee, for example, come from places such as India and South America; bananas and other exotic fruit can come from lovely islands in the Caribbean; chocolate comes from countries in Africa and Central America. All of these places are very hot and often very poor.

When we go shopping, we like to buy food that is cheap – food that doesn't cost us very much. But if we don't pay enough for our food when we buy it, then the poor farmers who work so hard to grow the food for us can't earn enough money to feed their families. Listen to some of the people that grow these foods:

© Badger Learning

Banana Grower 1

I grow bananas on a large plantation in Central America. The man who owns the plantation does not pay us much money. On top of that, he sprays the bananas with horrible chemicals, which means that many of us, including our children, become ill.

Banana Grower 2

I grow bananas on a big plantation too. A little while ago we joined **Fair Trade**, and life has become much better for us. Our pay has increased, which means we can afford things such as water and electricity. Chemicals are not used on the plantation now and weeds are pulled up by hand. This means that we are all healthier and happier.

Cocoa Grower 1

I grow cocoa. When the price of cocoa goes down we have to make some very difficult decisions such as should we send our children to school? Who should we buy medicine for? We can't afford to keep our crops healthy, so we produce less. It all means that our families suffer. But there is nothing else we can do.

Cocoa Grower 2

I am a cocoa grower as well, but we belong to **Fair Trade** now. We sell our cocoa through Fair Trade, which has made a big difference. We know that the chocolate company is going to give us a fair price and with the extra money we have been able to have concrete floors in our house instead of dirt. We can also send our children to secondary school so we know they have a future.

Which people were better off? Every time you heard Fair Trade mentioned, the families had a much better life, didn't they? That's because several years ago people realised that many growers in different countries were having a very difficult time, mainly because we want to buy cheap food. So the Fair Trade Foundation was set up to help these growers and farmers. They make sure that the farmers are paid a fair price for what they grow, and get paid a fair amount of money for their hard work. More and more organisations are now becoming part of the Fair Trade Foundation and products are easily available in supermarkets and shops.

So, the situation is being put right slowly, but it does depend on us and the choices we make at the supermarket. So, next time you are shopping with your family, look out for the Fair Trade sign and tell them about it. Every time you buy something with this sign you are helping a family to afford to feed themselves, have better housing, have proper medical care and send their children to school. It's something worth thinking about, isn't it?

Interactive Follow-Up Activities

Questions

Use a visualiser to go through the following questions with the children.

Fair Trade means:	Yes	No
Farmers get a fair price for their crops		
Workers have good housing		
Parents can afford to send their children to school		
Help is given so that harmful chemicals aren't used		
Workers have healthier lives		

Getting the message

1. Why was the Fair Trade Foundation set up? *(To ensure farmers and growers received a fair wage and a fair price for their crops)*.
2. What differences has Fair Trade made to many farmers and growers? *(Better housing, better wages, better health, better education)*.
3. How can we help? *(By choosing Fair Trade products more when we go shopping)*.
4. Put up your hand if:
   - You recognise the Fair Trade sign.
   - You know your family has bought Fair Trade products from the shops.
   - You're going to ask your family to look for Fair Trade products next time you go shopping.

Non-interactive Follow-Up

Summary

- Fair Trade was set up to ensure growers get a fair wage and a fair price for their goods.
- Fair Trade has had a direct impact on the lives of the farmers, including better housing; better education and better health.
- The Fair Trade foundation is growing rapidly.
- Fair Trade products are easily obtainable in supermarkets and shops.

Reflection

The choices we make can directly affect the lives of other people. We can help them simply by choosing more carefully when we go shopping.

Prayer

Lord God, thank You for the people who set up the Fair Trade Foundation and for the improvements that have been made to many people's lives. Help us to make wise choices so that we too can help people less fortunate than ourselves. Amen.

Objective
To help children understand the importance of the Christian communion service.

RE themes
Christianity, beliefs and practice, what happens in a church.

Props
(Not essential): a piece of bread and a communion cup.

Introduction
Have you ever wondered what it must be like on the moon? Well, some people have really been there. They found out it wasn't made of cheese, too. When they went there, they did something very special....

True Story: The Service on the Moon

A few years before your parents were born, everyone around the world who had a television sat down to watch a special event. A giant space rocket, taller than a house or a tree or a block of flats and nearly as tall as a skyscraper, was ready to blast off. Inside the rocket were three very nervous men – they were astronauts and they were going to fly to the moon.

"10, 9, 8, 7, 6, 5, 4, 3, 2, 1 we have lift off," said the voice. Suddenly there was a gigantic roar and a huge cloud of orange flame and white smoke boomed out from the rocket's engines. Slowly and quite gracefully, the massive white rocket rose into the sky. It went faster and faster as it lifted, then suddenly it shot into the clouds and disappeared from sight. In a few minutes it was in space. Everyone watching 'ooed' and clapped and cheered – it was very exciting.

After an hour, the astronauts could look out of the window of their spacecraft, which was fixed to the top of the rocket. They looked down at a most beautiful and amazing sight: a great blue ball, dotted with patterns of swirling white and patches of green and brown. It was the Earth, our own planet, hanging in space and turning gently. The three men radioed back to base to say they could see oceans and deserts and cities and jungles and how wonderful they looked from thousands of miles away in space.

It took a long time to reach the moon, even though the rocket was blasting along at over 20,000 miles per hour. When at last they were near to the moon's surface, the spaceship separated from the big rocket and flew around the moon to find the best place to land. The astronauts looked out of their little window once more and gasped with amazement. They saw a dusty grey surface covered with rocks and hills and craters, some tiny and some giant ones bigger than football pitches. They were the very first people ever to see these sights up close.

The spaceship's computer found the right place to land, where it was flat and not too rocky. Then the special landing craft descended down to the moon, taking two of the astronauts, while the third astronaut flew around the moon in the spaceship. It was a worrying moment for the two men, Buzz Aldrin and Neil Armstrong, because their landing craft was nearly out of fuel. But they soon felt a gentle bump and they knew that they had landed.

Before they went out onto the surface of the moon, the two men did something very special. They thanked God. They prayed, giving thanks that they had landed safely on the moon after a long and dangerous voyage. Next, they found three little plastic packages and opened them. There was a small cup given to Buzz by the people at his church, a tiny bottle of wine and two pieces of bread. The two men then held a communion service on the moon. This is something that happens in churches all over the world every Sunday. They ate the bread and drank the tiny cup of wine to remember that Jesus had died for them on the cross. Even on the moon, they wanted to remember how important this was.

Neil Armstrong, wearing his spacesuit, was the first man to step onto the moon. What a moment! The surface was soft and dusty, and his boots left clear footprints – which are still there today. Buzz soon joined Neil on the surface and the pictures of this moment are still remembered by everyone who saw them on that day.

Buzz and Neil prayed for a safe journey back and two days later they were safely back on Earth. It had been quite an adventure!

Interactive Follow-Up Activities

Questions
1. Where was the rocket going? *(To the moon).*
2. What did the astronauts see when they looked out of the window of the spacecraft? *(The Earth and the moon).*
3. What did Neil Armstrong and Buzz Aldrin do on the moon? *(They held a communion service; they prayed and gave thanks for their journey).*

Getting the message
1. Why did the two men take bread and wine onto the moon? *(They held a service to give thanks to God and to remember that Jesus died on the cross).*
1. What do you think it felt like to be so far from the Earth? Why did the astronauts pray? *(Because it was a very dangerous journey; they wanted God to look after them on the way home).*
3. Put your hand up if...
   - You'd be brave enough to go to the moon.
   - You'd like to be an astronaut.
   - You'd like to go into space and look down on the Earth.
   - You'd rather stay safe and sound on this planet.
   - You'd pray for a safe journey home if you were on the moon.

Non-interactive Follow-Up

Summary of the story

- Three astronauts went in a giant rocket to the moon more than thirty years ago.
- They saw the Earth from space and it looked very beautiful.
- Their space craft landed on the moon and two of them stepped onto the moon's surface.
- They held a special communion service to give thanks for their mission.
- They prayed for a safe journey home.
- They returned to Earth safely.

Reflection

The three astronauts who went to the moon looked down from space and saw the planet Earth. They saw that it was beautiful and amazing and they knew that we must all look after it because it is our home. They also knew that they needed to say thanks for their wonderful journey. Try to remember to say thanks next time someone takes you somewhere exciting.

Prayer

Lord God, thank You for the Earth and the moon. They are both wonderful and beautiful. Help us to look after them. Also we thank You that You took care of the astronauts who flew to the moon and thank You for all the safe journeys that we have, even the short ones. Amen.

Objective

To help children understand how people's faith can give them hope and comfort in times of distress.

RE themes

Christianity, beliefs and practice, prayer.

Props

(Not essential): a bottle of water.

Introduction

Water is so easy for us to get hold of that we don't really think about how important it is. Here's a remarkable true story which shows that water is truly precious.

True Story: Ocean Rescue

Donna was really excited when she saw the big ship waiting at the harbour in the summer of 1942.

"That's the ship that's going to take us back to America," said her father. Donna wondered what America was like. She had lived in Africa for as long as she could remember, which wasn't very long, since she was only seven years old.

"Why are we going to America daddy?" said Donna.

"Because it's not safe for us here in Africa – there's a big war going on around the world and there may be fighting here soon."

Donna's father was talking about World War II. He didn't want to leave the villages or the people he worked with but he knew that he had to take his family to a safer place. He worked as a Christian missionary among the people of West Africa – a missionary is a person who travels around, telling people about Jesus and the message of the Bible. Now, he was boarding a big ship with his wife, son and daughter to go to another new life.

The journey was exciting for Donna and her brother Richard. The ship rolled over big waves as it crossed the mighty Atlantic Ocean. Donna enjoyed standing on the deck and watching the birds swooping overhead. The children had no idea just how dangerous their voyage was going to be.

After several days sailing, the ship was getting close to the Caribbean Sea. The weather was warm and it looked like it was going to be another quiet day. Donna was on the upper deck as usual, playing with her brother when suddenly, completely unexpectedly, there was the most enormous explosion. The ship lurched sideways and Donna was thrown off her feet. She landed badly and didn't realise that she had broken a bone in her arm. There was a great cloud of smoke and sparks and people were screaming.

Donna didn't know what to do. She looked around for her brother, Richard and saw him sliding down the deck away from her. Then she realised that he was sliding because the ship was leaning over. She heard someone shout, "submarine attack". A few moments later Donna found herself in the water – she had fallen into the Atlantic Ocean as the ship began to sink. The water was cold but Donna didn't panic because Richard was still with her and they were both good swimmers. Her brother called to her to follow him towards a small boat they could see nearby.

Donna didn't realise it at the time, but the ship had been hit by a torpedo fired by a German submarine. The Germans were sinking ships in the ocean to stop weapons and food reaching Europe.

The boat that Richard had seen turned out be a life raft made of wood and oil drums. It was already full of people when the two children reached it, but strong arms pulled them up on board out of the water. Donna turned round to look at the ship but it had already gone. Then she looked around the raft for her mother and father. They were not there. It later turned out that Donna's father had swum to another raft, but she never knew what happened to her mother.

There were nineteen people on the flimsy life raft altogether. It was designed to hold just ten. Water seeped in between the wooden poles and everyone was cold and shocked by what had happened. There was no sail or engine to power the raft and so it just drifted on the sea. A kind-looking woman put an arm round Donna and said that they would be rescued soon by another ship. She explained that there was water and some food on the raft too.

It soon grew dark and there was no sign of a rescue ship. No one had a radio or telephone. Donna was scared and clung to her big brother for comfort. The days passed. Soon the food began to run out and each person was only allowed a small amount of water. Donna was sunburnt and hungry. She also heard someone mention that there were sharks around the raft and Richard told her not to dangle her hands over the side.

The people on the raft were quiet for most of the time to save energy, but some of them wailed out loud at their misfortune, while others sobbed. There were three people, however, who seemed calmer than the others. They were Christians, like Donna's family, and they spent their time on the raft comforting others and praying. After a few more days at sea, everyone began to pray, including Donna. They called out to God to save them and send a rescue ship soon.

After twenty-one days, when the water and food were almost gone, someone spied a ship in the distance. There was great excitement on the raft and everyone began to wave and shout. Then the survivors heard a whistling sound followed by a crashing boom. The ship was a warship and it had just fired its guns at the raft! The people waved and screamed and then the guns stopped. The ship turned towards the raft, realising that it wasn't a submarine.

Donna, Richard and the other people were rescued safely by the sailors on board the British warship and were taken to the nearest island. As they stepped onto dry land the people were still praying, thanking God for rescuing them from peril on the sea.

Interactive Follow-Up Activities

Questions
1. Why was Donna's family going to America on board a ship? *(Because there was a war on and they had to leave Africa).*
2. What happened to the ship? *(It was torpedoed by a submarine and sank).*
3. What happened to Donna after the ship sank? *(She swam to a raft; the raft drifted at sea for twenty-one days, then it was rescued by another ship).*

Getting the message
1. Why did some of the people on the raft pray? *(They were Christians who believed that God would help them; they wanted to be rescued).*
2. How would you feel if you were stuck on a raft at sea?
3. True or false? Put your thumb up if I say something true about the story; put your thumb down if I say something that's not true:
   - The people on the raft all knew each other. *(F)*
   - Donna and her brother had to swim to the raft. *(T)*
   - Being on the raft was good fun. *(F)*
   - Some people on the raft prayed to God for help. *(T)*
   - The Christians helped the other people on the raft. *(T)*

Non-interactive Follow-Up

Summary of the story

- Donna was seven years old in 1942 during World War II.
- Her family had to go by ship to America from Africa, where her father was a Christian missionary.
- The ship was torpedoed in the Atlantic by a German submarine.
- Donna and her brother Richard managed to swim to a wooden life raft despite Donna's broken arm; the ship sank.
- The children were separated from their parents; the raft had ninteen people aboard.
- They drifted at sea for twenty-one days, short of food and water and surrounded by sharks.
- The survivors were rescued by a British warship after it had initially fired on them.

Reflection

It is good that we live in times of peace and not war. Remember the bravery of those people who suffered terribly in World War II, such as Donna and her brother. Be grateful too that we always have fresh water to drink.

Prayer

Lord God, thank You that You rescued Donna and those other brave people who were adrift at sea on a wooden raft for three weeks. Thank You that You answered their prayers. Help us to remember to pray and to say thanks for the peace we have and all that You give us. Amen.

21 Chocolate Spread

Objective
To help children understand the importance of prayer to Christians, and also of giving and sharing.

RE themes
Christianity, beliefs and practice, prayer, helping others.

Props
(Not essential): a jar of chocolate spread.

Introduction
Who likes chocolate spread? Mmmm, it's gorgeous isn't it? A real treat. Well, today's assembly begins with a true story all about chocolate spread....

True Story: Chocolate Spread

Disa was fed up. She looked through the big cardboard box once more, just to check. Beans, pasta, breakfast cereal, more pasta, tuna, tins of soup and some digestive biscuits. She didn't even like digestive biscuits. Disa was just trudging off to her bedroom when mum came into the kitchen.

"What's up, precious? You look miserable."

"I've just had a look through the food box – it's all the same old stuff that we always get."

"Well Disa, I'm sorry the food isn't very exciting but remember, we don't choose it – all this comes from the people at church – it's what they give us."

"But why do we have food boxes from church mum? Most people don't have them."

"That's a good question – maybe I'd better explain it to you properly."

Disa sat down with her mum and listened. Mum explained how dad had suddenly lost his job two months ago and that the family now had a lot less money than before. They had to stop buying all sorts of things, including expensive food. She told Disa that they still had to pay for the house and things such as electricity, gas, water, the telephone and clothes. Disa said she just didn't think it was fair.

"There are many people much worse off than we are Disa," said Mum. "Anyway, I'm sure Dad will get another job soon and until then, we can be thankful that the people in our church are kind enough to bring food to share."

"But why don't they bring something nice? Why is it always pasta and beans? Why doesn't anyone bring chocolate spread?"

Mum laughed. "Well, that would be nice, but chocolate spread is not cheap, Disa. Let's wait until next week and see what we get – you never know, the box might have something more exciting in it."

The following Sunday, Disa went to church with her mum, Dad and brother, Ben. She loved going because it was always fun. For a start, they didn't actually meet in an old church building at all – the meetings were in a huge secondary school. They had songs with a band on stage in the big hall first, then all the children went to different rooms where they had stories and activities. There were toys and lots of things to do, like drawing and playing games. At the end, Disa was collected by her mum or dad and then they went to pick up their food box from a man called Phil. Disa was desperate to see what was in the box when dad returned with it.

"Wait until you get home miss," said Dad.

When they did get home, Disa helped unpack the box. Beans, breakfast cereal, pasta, packet soup, tuna, more beans. Oh it was nearly all the same again. There was no chocolate spread or anything nice. Disa went into her bedroom. As she lay on her bed, she remembered what Mrs Brennan had said at church about how good it was to pray to God every day.

"Oh please God. Can we have some chocolate spread?" said Disa. Then she remembered to thank God for her family and her home and asked Him to help her dad find a job.

Next Sunday, the children performed a little play for the adults at church in the main hall. Disa was playing the part of Noah's wife. It was such good fun that she forgot all about the food box. When she got home, her brother Ben brought the box into the kitchen and started emptying it. The first thing he brought out was a packet of pasta. Then he said, "Ooh," and reached into the box. In his hand was a jar of chocolate spread! Disa couldn't believe it.

"Mum, did you or dad tell someone at church to put that in the box?"

"Of course not, dear – you can't do that."

"But Mum, last week I prayed for chocolate spread!"

Mum laughed. "Well it looks like your prayers have been answered."

But the story doesn't end there. While Disa and Ben were busy tucking into chocolate spread on toast later that week, the man who led their church, a minister called Frank, was on board an aeroplane, flying to Switzerland. He had been invited to talk about the church to a big group of Christians. Frank told them all about the food boxes, which were a great success. He also told them about Disa and her prayer – he knew because Disa's mum had phoned to tell him what had happened.

Another week later, Frank was back from Switzerland. Unexpectedly, he came round to Disa's house.

"I can't stay long," he said. "I just wanted to pass on this to the little girl of the family." It was a square parcel wrapped in brown paper. It had Disa's name on the front. While she opened the package, Frank explained who it was from. "An old lady came to see me in Switzerland, after I did my talk about the food boxes. She said she loved the story of the little girl and the chocolate spread, and she wanted to give me this for the family, but she said the girl must open it."

Disa had now opened it. It was the biggest jar of chocolate spread she, or anyone in the room, had ever seen. It was enormous! "And that's Swiss chocolate spread too," said Frank. "They make the best chocolate in the world." And when Disa tasted it, she just had to agree.

Interactive Follow-Up Activities

Questions
1. Why was Disa fed up at the start of the story? *(Because her family kept getting the same food in the boxes given by people at church)*.
2. Who did Disa ask for chocolate spread? *(God – she prayed)*.
3. Why did Disa get another big jar of chocolate spread? *(A lady in Switzerland gave it, after she heard about Disa)*.

Getting the message
1. Why did people at Disa's church bring food along each week? *(To give to people who didn't have much money)*.
2. Do you think Disa would get chocolate spread every week if she prayed for it? *(Probably not; Christians don't believe that God always gives us what we want)*.
3. Call out the right word to finish off these sentences about the story:
   - Disa's family were given boxes of _____. *(food)*
   - The food was given by people at Disa's _____. *(church)*
   - Disa wanted some chocolate _____. *(spread)*
   - Disa prayed to _____. *(God)*
   - A lady gave them another jar of chocolate spread which was very _____. *(big)*

Non-interactive Follow-Up

Summary of the story

- Disa's family received food boxes from church because they were short of money.
- Disa was fed up with always getting the same food, such as pasta and beans.
- Disa prayed that they would get some chocolate spread.
- A jar of chocolate spread arrived in the next box.
- A lady in Switzerland heard the story and gave the family a huge jar of chocolate spread.

Reflection

Remember next time you want something that there is always someone worse off than you. Try to give and to share like the people at Disa's church. Try to help others whenever you can.

Prayer

Lord God, thank You for answering Disa's prayer. Help us to remember that we shouldn't just pray for lots of things that we want. Help us instead to pray for other people and to share what we have, like the people at Disa's church sharing their food. Amen.

Objective

To help children understand the Christian message that it is important to treat others as we ourselves like to be treated.

RE themes

Christianity, beliefs and practice, helping others.
For more information on the charity mentioned in the story, visit
http://operationchristmaschild.org.uk/

Props

A Barbie doll and a shoebox covered in Christmas wrapping paper.

Introduction

Who loves getting presents? It's really exciting when you get something that you've been wanting for a long while. Here's a true story about a little girl who wanted something very badly. Listen carefully to find out what happened.

Story: Natalie's Dolls

Natalie wanted a Barbie doll. She'd wanted one for ages and ages. When she'd opened her birthday presents last week, she was really pleased with the toys she'd got, but she'd been a bit disappointed that there hadn't been a Barbie. She tried not to let her mum notice that she was a bit sad, because she loved her mum, and Natalie knew that her mum had done her best to make her birthday nice. She still managed to enjoy her birthday, though, because she had a lovely party with all her friends.

One day, when she came home from school, Natalie saw a big pile of shoeboxes in the corner of the kitchen.

"Wow! Have you been buying loads of shoes, Mum?" asked Natalie.

Mum laughed, "No – what would I do with that many all at once? I've just been to the shoe shop and asked for lots of empty shoeboxes. Do you remember at church on Sunday, when they were telling us about all those poor children from other countries who don't have toys or even homes or families?"

Natalie did remember. She'd felt very sad when she'd heard all about children who were so poor that they'd never been given a present – ever. Not even for Christmas or their birthday.

"Well," said Mum, "There's a charity that has thought of a really clever idea. They are asking people in this country to share some of their things with these children."

"But how can we do that?" asked Natalie. "We don't know them – we don't even know where they live, to send them things!"

"They've thought of that. What we do is to cover some shoe boxes with Christmas wrapping paper, to make them look just like presents, and then we fill them with little things that we think a child might like. Things like cuddly toys, dolls, paper and pencils, sweets, picture books and hats and gloves: just the sort of things that you'd like too. When the boxes are full, we'll take them to the church, and then someone will take all of the boxes that the church has collected to a place where hundreds and hundreds of other boxes are brought along. Then a giant lorry will take them to the other countries where the children are waiting for them, in time for Christmas."

"What a good idea!" said Natalie. "Can I help you fill the boxes?"

"Of course," smiled Mum. "I've bought some nice things already, but maybe you can find some things in your bedroom that you wouldn't mind giving to a poor boy or girl who doesn't have anything. Don't get anything old and tatty, though – we don't want to make them think that they only deserve rotten old toys that nobody else wants any more. If you're not sure which things to pick, just ask yourself if you'd be pleased to get them as a present. They're only good enough for someone else if they're good enough for you! A really good rule to remember is always to treat other people in just the same way as you'd like to be treated yourself. That's one of the most important things that Jesus tells us in The Bible."

So off Natalie went, and soon came back with an armful of nice things for the boxes. In no time they had filled three and a half boxes. Just then, there was a knock on the door. It was Nasreen from next door, and she was carrying a bag.

"Hi there you two! I heard your church was collecting things to put in shoeboxes for children in countries such as Russia and Romania. I wanted to do one too, but I haven't got the time to get a box and cover it. I wonder if you could fit these few things into one of your boxes?"

"Thanks, Nasreen!" said Mum. "We've got a big gap in one of our boxes, so that's perfect. We'll pop your things in with ours."

When Nasreen had gone, Natalie opened the bag, and what do you think was inside? In the bag were two beautiful Barbie dolls, and even some clothes to go with them.

"Oh, Mum, look!" she gasped. "That's just like the one I'd love to have!"

It was very hard for Natalie to put the dolls and all their beautiful clothes into the box. She even thought to herself, "Maybe I could put just one in, and keep the other one…" but then she thought that that wouldn't be fair at all. After all, she had so many nice toys, and the poor children in Romania had nothing. So, she gave a little sigh and laid the dolls into the box carefully. It made her smile to think how excited one little girl would be when she opened her shoebox in a far away country at Christmas time. Mum was very proud of her.

There's a wonderful ending to this true story, too. For a start, the little girl who got the shoebox with the dolls in was very excited and pleased, but do you know what else happened? On Christmas Day, in among Natalie's presents was a beautiful Barbie doll! Mum smiled as she watched Natalie opening the wrapping paper and shouting with excitement.

"You see, Natalie," she said, "I know how hard it was for you to send those Barbies to someone else, when that was the one thing you really wanted for yourself. But you truly did treat that little girl in a far away place just as you would like to be treated yourself. And this is your reward!"

Natalie hugged her mum and played with her doll all day long.

Interactive Follow-Up Activities

Questions
1. What was the one toy that Natalie really wanted? *(A Barbie doll).*
2. There was a big pile of something in the corner of Natalie's kitchen. Put your hand up if you think it was:
   a. newspapers
   b. washing
   c. shoeboxes ✓
3. What were the shoeboxes for? *(For filling with gifts and sending to poor children who don't have toys, families or even homes).*
4. What did Nasreen have in her bag? Put your hand on your head if you think it was:
   a. a toy racing car
   b. a Barbie doll
   c. TWO Barbie dolls and some clothes ✓

Getting the message
1. Natalie's mum said it was important to treat other people in the same way that you'd like to be treated yourself. How did Natalie do that? *(She put the Barbies into the shoebox for the poor little girl, even though she really wanted a Barbie herself).*
2. Think of some of the things we would do for others if we treated them as we would like to be treated. Hands up if you can think of something. *(Sharing, being kind, taking turns).*
3. What about things we wouldn't do if we treated other people as we would like to be treated? *(Lying, cheating, saying horrid things, pushing in, not letting people join in games).*

Non-interactive Follow-Up

Summary of the story
- Natalie wanted a Barbie doll.
- Natalie's mum had heard of a charity that sent presents to poor children in other countries.
- Natalie and mum filled shoeboxes with gifts for the children.
- Nasreen gave them two Barbie dolls to put into the shoeboxes.
- Natalie was tempted to keep one of the dolls for herself, but put both into the boxes in the end.
- Mum was very proud of her because she had treated the little girl who was to get the doll just as she would have liked to have been treated herself.
- Natalie got a Barbie doll for Christmas.

Reflection
Sometimes it's hard to do the right thing and not to be selfish or mean. If you're not sure what to do, always try thinking about how the other person will feel. Jesus told us always to treat other people just how we would like to be treated ourselves. It's not always easy to do it, though!

Prayer
Lord God, thank You that Jesus told us so many useful things. It's such a good idea to treat other people just how we'd like to be treated ourselves. Help us never to do anything that we wouldn't like someone else to do to us. Amen.

Objective
To help children understand that retaliation usually makes situations worse.

RE themes
Christianity, beliefs and practice, forgiveness.

Props
(None).

Preparation
This assembly is in the form of a simple play or sketch for two children (G, a girl and B, a boy) and the teacher (T). Both children will need to be good, confident readers with clear voices. The play will need to be rehearsed before the assembly but it is suggested that the scripts should be used all the way through.

Introduction
Today's assembly is a short, simple play about arguments.

Play: The Argument

G	I'm going to tell the teacher!
B	You started it!
T	Right – calm down you two and tell me what happened.
G	Well, he borrowed my ruler and when it came back there was writing on it.
B	But I've told you, I didn't write on it – someone else did it.
T	Who did the writing?
B	I don't know but it wasn't me.
G	It must have been you!
B	I didn't do anything, but you scribbled on my picture.
T	Did that really happen?
G	Yes, but only because he wrote on my ruler.
B	I keep telling you, it wasn't me!
T	And what happened next?
G	Well he bent the cover of my book.
B	Only because you spoiled my picture.
G	Well you deserved it.
T	It sounds to me like you're both to blame.
B	But I didn't do anything.
G	You did – you bent my new book.
B	But you started it.
G	No I didn't – you did – you borrowed my ruler.
T	Stop now, both of you. I don't know exactly what happened at the beginning to start this, but now both of you are doing things that you know are wrong.

B	But...
T	Just listen.
G	But...
T	Let me tell you a true story. There was once a husband and wife who had an argument about a cup of coffee. The man said the woman spilt it and the woman said the man spilt it. Well, they argued all day and all night until they just stopped talking to each other. The next day they still didn't say a word – neither one would give in.
B	What happened next?
T	Well they started sleeping in separate bedrooms and they avoided each other all the time, never saying a word.
G	But they must have talked sometimes?
T	No, never – they left each other little notes on pieces of paper occasionally, that's all. Soon they divided the house completely in two: the man had one half and the woman had the other half. They lived completely separate lives in the same house. And they were both miserable for the rest of their lives.
B	Is that really true?
T	Yes it happened in America, in the last century.
G	But it was only about a cup of coffee.
T	Yes, two people's lives were ruined because of an argument.
B	If only one of them had said sorry.
T	Yes, it's just one little word, easy to say.
G	I suppose we'd better say it too, after our argument.
B	Sorry.
G	Sorry.
T	Well done, and next time don't get into an argument at all. Jesus taught that you shouldn't fight back but always make your peace with someone as soon as you can.

Interactive Follow-Up Activities

Questions

1. What were the two children arguing about? *(Writing on a ruler, drawing on a picture, bending a book; they were blaming each other and retaliating).*

2. Did the girl scribbling on the boy's drawing make the situation better or worse? *(Worse – up to then she hadn't done anything wrong; after this they were both in the wrong).*

3. Why did the teacher tell them a story? *(So they could see what trouble not saying sorry can lead to; to teach them a lesson).*

Getting the message

1. What can we learn from the story of the man and woman and the cup of coffee? *(To say sorry, to not let things get out of hand; sometimes it's better to apologise even if it's not your fault; don't retaliate or you'll make things worse)*.

2. What happens if people keep trying to get their own back, like the girl and the boy? *(Things just get worse; both people get into trouble; it can turn into a fight)*.

3. Here are some things you could do if you get into an argument.
   - You can just stop and walk away or keep quiet. Hands up who would do that?
   - You can go and tell a teacher. Hands up who would do that?
   - If you know you are right, you can carry on arguing. Hands up who would do that?
   - If the person does something bad to you, you can do something bad back to them. Hands up who would do that?
   - You can stop the argument right away by saying sorry. Hands up who would do that?

Non-interactive Follow-Up

Summary of the story
- Two children were arguing about a ruler.
- They both made the argument worse by doing things to annoy each other.
- The teacher stopped them and told them a story about a married couple.
- They argued about a cup of coffee and stopped talking to each other.
- Eventually, they divided the house in two and lived separate lives in the same house, and were miserable for ever more.
- The children realised that they needed to stop arguing and say sorry.

Reflection
Arguing usually gets you nowhere. Trying to do something back to a person who has annoyed you often makes things worse. When you get into a situation where someone has upset you, try to stay calm, try not to argue back but leave things as they are. That way you won't get blamed.

Prayer
Lord God, help us not to get into arguments. Help us not to fight back against people who upset us but to stay calm and not make matters worse. Help us to think what to say and do in these situations. Amen.

24 The Ten Plagues

Objective
To familiarise children with one of the most famous Old Testament stories.

RE themes
Judaism, The Torah, Bible stories, Old Testament, Moses.

Props
(Not essential): a wooden staff or walking stick.

Preparation
This assembly is in the form of a simple play suitable for a Y2 or mixed Y1/Y2 class. Four good readers are needed to play the parts of Narrators (N1 and N2), Moses and Pharaoh. The remainder of the class can mime the ten plagues and play Egyptians and Israelites, too. Explain the background to the story and allow all the readers to use the script.

Introduction
Today's assembly is a short, simple play that tells the story of the Ten Plagues from the Bible.

Play: The Ten Plagues

N1   This story takes place a long, long time ago, in the country of Egypt, when the pyramids had just been built and Pharaoh ruled the land.

N2   The people of Israel lived in Egypt at that time. But they were not free – they were all slaves. They had to work hard all day without any money. They were often treated very badly by their Egyptian masters.

N1   The leader of the slaves was Moses.

Moses   Pharaoh! Let my people go – they want to go back to Israel.
Pharaoh   These people are my slaves, I will never let them go.
Moses   But Pharaoh, God has sent me. He says let my people go!
Pharaoh   My answer is no.
Moses   God says that if you do not set the slaves free, he will punish you. He will send plagues on your land.
Pharaoh   Go away Moses – you are just a troublemaker.

N1   So Moses went away and God sent him down to the River Nile.
N2   When Moses put his wooden staff into the water, the river turned to blood!

Moses   Pharaoh, let my people go!
Pharaoh   I will not.

© Badger Learning

N1	So God sent Moses to the ponds and streams.
N2	When Moses held out his wooden staff, millions of frogs came out of the water.
N1	They went into people's houses and into Pharaoh's palace and they jumped on the Egyptians.

Moses	Pharaoh, let my people go!
Pharaoh	No!

N1	So God sent Moses into the desert.
N2	When Moses held out his staff over the sand, the sand turned into gnats.
N1	The insects buzzed around the Egyptians and bit them.

Moses	Pharaoh, let my people go!
Pharaoh	Never!

N1	So after this God sent a plague of flies on the Egyptian people.

Moses	Pharaoh, let my people go!
Pharaoh	These slaves belong to me – stop asking this question!

N1	So God sent Moses to warn Pharaoh that there would be a plague on the Egyptian's animals.
N2	The next day, all of the Egyptians' cows and sheep and camels were dead.

Moses	Pharaoh, let my people go!
Pharaoh	They are my slaves – they will stay here.

N1	So God told Moses to throw soot into the air.
N2	When the soot landed on the Egyptians, terrible boils appeared on their skin.

Moses	Pharaoh, let my people go!
Pharaoh	I will not do it.

N1	So God told Moses to stretch out his hand towards the sky.
N2	Then there was a powerful hailstorm.
N1	The giant hailstones flattened all of the Egyptians' corn so that they had nothing to eat.

Moses	Pharaoh, let my people go!
Pharaoh	They are going nowhere Moses.

N1	Then God told Moses to stretch out his hand over the land.
N2	This time a great plague of locusts appeared, like a giant cloud.
N1	These insects ate anything that was green in the land.

Moses	Pharaoh, let my people go!
Pharaoh	No, no, no!

N1	So God told Moses to stretch out his hand towards the sky.
N2	Then a terrible darkness fell over Egypt.

N1	It was completely dark for three days.
Moses	Pharaoh, let my people go!
Pharaoh	You cannot make me.
N1	Then God sent Moses to warn Pharaoh that if he did not let the people of Israel go, there would be one last plague.
N2	This plague would be much more terrible than the rest.
N1	When Pharaoh would not listen, the eldest son of every family in Egypt died in the night.
N2	Pharaoh's son, the prince, died too.
Moses	Pharaoh, let my people go!
Pharaoh	Leave my people. Go from here, for I know now that your God loves you and your people.
N1	And so the people of Israel were no longer slaves.
N2	They went across the desert and headed back to their homes in Israel.

Interactive Follow-Up Activities

Questions
1. Who was the ruler of Egypt? *(The Pharaoh)*.
2. Why didn't he want to let the slaves from Israel go? *(Because they did a lot of his hard work)*.
3. What were the plagues that God sent to help Moses? *(River turning to blood, frogs, gnats, flies, animals dying, boils, hail, locusts, darkness, death of the firstborn)*.

Getting the message
1. What would you have done if you had been Pharaoh?
2. Put your hand up if you agree with each of these statements:
   - It was wrong for the Egyptians to keep slaves.
   - God gave Pharaoh lots of chances to set the people of Israel free.
   - The plagues were Moses' own idea.
   - The Egyptians always treated their slaves kindly.
   - Pharaoh should have let the slaves go right at the beginning.

Non-interactive Follow-Up

Summary of the story
- The people of Israel were slaves in Egypt.
- Moses, their leader asked Pharaoh to let his people go.
- God told Moses to warn Pharaoh that he would send plagues on the land.
- Pharaoh still would not let the Israelites go.
- God sent ten plagues, and each time Moses asked Pharaoh to let the people go.
- The plagues were: River Nile turning to blood, frogs, gnats, flies, animals dying, boils, hail, locusts, darkness, death of the firstborn.
- Only after his own son died did Pharaoh set the people free.

Reflection
Pharaoh was very stubborn. He let his people suffer an awful lot before he would set the Israeli people free. Sometimes we don't do something when we know it is right. Try to avoid trouble and always do what is right straight away.

Prayer
Lord God, help us not to be stubborn like Pharaoh was. He let his people and his land suffer because he would not change his mind. Help us to do what we know is right, even when it doesn't suit us. Amen.

25 I Found a Pound

Objective
To help children think about the importance of being honest.

RE themes
Christianity, beliefs and practice.

Props
(Not essential): a pound coin.

Introduction
Have you ever found some money on the pavement or in the playground? Well, today's assembly starts with a poem about someone who did just that.

Poem: I Found a Pound

I found a pound;
I went to the shops and walked around.

I went to the shops and walked around;
I bought some sweets with the money I found.

I bought some sweets with the money I found;
I took them home and passed them round.

I took them home and passed them round;
I saw my sister looking at the ground.

I saw my sister looking at the ground;
I asked my sister why she frowned.

I asked my sister why she frowned;
She said she was looking for a pound.

She said she was looking for a pound;
She said she dropped it on the ground.

She said she dropped it on the ground;
She said she hoped it would be found.

She said she hoped it would be found;
She said it must be somewhere around.

She said it must be somewhere around;
I thought shall I tell her about the pound?

I thought shall I tell her about the pound?
I thought should I tell her it has been found?

© Badger Learning

I thought should I tell her it has been found?
I thought shall I tell her I went into town?

I thought shall I tell her I went into town?
But instead I left her and turned around.

Instead I left her and turned around;
I crept to the house without a sound.

I crept to the house without a sound;
I went to my room and looked for a pound.

I went to my room and looked for a pound;
I searched my pockets until one was found.

I searched my pockets until one was found;
I went outside where my sister still frowned.

I went outside where my sister still frowned;
I pretended to search across the ground.

I pretended to search across the ground;
I knelt right down upon a small mound.

I knelt right down upon a small mound;
And out of my pocket I took the pound.

Out of my pocket I took the pound;
And carefully I placed it down.

Carefully I placed it down;
I placed it where it was bound to be found.

I placed it where it was bound to be found;
Then I stood up straight and turned around.

I stood up straight and turned around;
Should I have told my sister I spent her pound?

Should I have told my sister I spent her pound?

Interactive Follow-Up Activities

Questions
1. What did the person who found the pound do with it? *(Bought some sweets at the shops)*.
2. Who did the pound belong to? *(The person's sister)*.
3. What did the person do in the house and afterwards? *(Found a pound of their/they own then put it outside for their sister to find)*.

Getting the message
1. Do you think the person did the right thing to replace the lost pound?
2. What should you do if you find some money?
3. Put your thumb up if you agree with these statements and put your thumb down if your disagree:
   - If you find some money you should give it to your parents or teacher.
   - Finders, keepers.
   - It's OK to keep a little bit of money if you find it but not a lot of money.
   - Keeping money that you've found is a little bit like stealing.
   - If you lose some money you should tell someone right away.

Non-interactive Follow-Up

Summary of the poem
   - The poet found a pound.
   - The pound was spent on sweets.
   - The poet's sister lost a pound.
   - The poet found a pound of his own and put it outside for his sister to find.
   - The poet wondered whether he should have told the truth.

Reflection
Remember that being honest is very, very important. If you find something that doesn't belong to you, you should not just keep it. Imagine how you would feel if someone else spent your money. Honesty is always best.

Prayer
Lord God, help us always to be honest in everything we do. Help us to remember to tell an adult if we find some money or something else that doesn't belong to us. Help us to always be truthful. Amen.

Badger Learning
Oldmedow Road,
Hardwick Industrial Estate,
King's Lynn,
PE30 4JJ
Tel: 01553 769209
Fax: 01553 767646

Badger Assembly Stories with Christian themes
Ages 5-7
ISBN 978 1 78147 929 2

Note: Due to the nature of the internet - it is vital that you check internet links before they are used in the class room.

Publisher: Susan Ross
Senior Editor: Danny Pearson
Designer: Adam Wilmott
Cover illustration: Adam Wilmott

Attempts to contact all copyright holders have been made. If any omitted would care to contact Badger Learning, we will be happy to make appropriate arrangements.

Printed in the UK